SPIRITUALITY AND HOLISTIC LIVING

Spirituality and Holistic Living

Sr Theresa Feist

MERCIER PRESS

MERCIER PRESS
PO Box 5, 5 French Church Street, Cork
16 Hume Street, Dublin 2

A CIP record for this book is available from the British Library.

ISBN 0 85342 932 4

FIRST PUBLISHED IN 1990

Reprinted in 1991, 1992, 1995

ACKNOWLEDGEMENTS

I wish to acknowledge the help of Mabel Fowler, who typed the manuscript, and the work of Adelene Joss, Teresa and Julien Buors, my assistants in compiling it. To John Fowler and Damien Loiselle, sincere thanks for providing excellent resources for the book. To Father Pat, whose devotion to life and truth has awakened the gift in hundreds of people, my deep gratitude. I would like to thank Spiros Lenis, Leo Schafer, Bernard Jensen, Lawrence Freeman and the Benedictine Priory of Montreal for permission to quote from their works.

Printed in Ireland by Colour Books Ltd.

Dedication

This book is dedicated to the priests and sisters of Ireland and anyone who is ready to hear the contents. The pages are inspired by discoveries of life in the past twenty-five years, beginning with a class in philosophy taken in Saskatoon under the professorship of Jim Penna .. and followed through with discoveries made in Ireland and France as recently as months before publication. There is no claim whatever to medical expertise.

Note

The information in this book is presented for educational value. It should in no way replace the normal medical diagnosis or treatment of disease, but may be used as an adjunct to the treatment of those diseases where appropriate.

Contents

'To be a religious means to seek, day after day, with fidelity and tenacity, *interior equilibrium*. . . it is a question of gradually and patiently coming to know what dwells within us, of harmonising the various components of our person which make us original and unrepeatable. Holiness passes by way of "the reconciliation of soul and body", as Theodoret affirms.' (*Therap XII*, 53)

POPE JOHN PAUL II

(From the text of the Holy Father's homily at the celebration of the Mass in the Syro-Marionite Rite, St Peter's Basilica, on 2 February 1988)

Foreword

Sister Theresa Feist is a tough, determined, open-minded healer whose only interest is in helping sick people recover, no matter how that is achieved. For her, as for all successful healers, the reason why a certain procedure is helpful is not nearly so important as the simple fact that it is helpful. This contrasts sharply with 'scientific' medicine, which places much more importance upon explanations and less upon actual therapeutic results.

Sister Theresa's healings are representative of natural healing. Apparently Hippocrates, around 400 BC, advanced a theory of healing based upon the body's natural adaptive powers. He called these the *physis*, a word adopted by the profession of physicians. *Physis* he described as a healing power or a self-adjusting power within the body. 'It is the vitality of nature that finds the way. . . to preserve a perfect equilibrium. . . to re-establish order and harmony.'

Hippocrates was opposed by Democritus who argued that everything could be explained by the atoms of which we are made and the forces exercised by and between them: he imagined no bodily healing power. Hippocrates, the first great physician whose name is synonymous with healing, espoused the concept of 'vitalism'. Democritus spoke of atomism. The debate still rages with physicians as the principal disciples of Democritus and healers as the main followers of Hippocrates. Would it not be interesting if the Hippocratic Oath included support of vitalism?

Sister Theresa's view represents healing which seeks to mobilise every positive force within the person to achieve health. This may include use of optimum nutrition, nutrient supplements, the principles of clinical ecology, light and colour therapy, magnetism, spirituality and meditation.

A healer must be optimistic and this sense of optimism must be conveyed to the sick. This Sister Theresa does very effectively. Without hope, it is very difficult for the body to marshal fully all of its defences against disease and destruction.

There are physicians who will not read this book, because it will not be reviewed in medical journals. They will not comprehend her message which is to do everything in one's power to bolster the body's defences, not only with those techniques that are said to be 'proven' by medical science. Some will disagree with her methods. But I know many good physicians who also use the techniques described by Sister Theresa: magnetism, colour and light therapy, acupuncture, and others. Whether or not they adopt these methods, they ought not to disbelieve the results she obtains.

I have known Sister Theresa since she first began to take Vitamin B3, and I consider her to be an accurate and honest reporter.

I do not pretend to understand how all of these therapeutic factors work, but then I find it equally difficult to understand how vitamins work, how antibiotics work, and in fact how a great many of the major therapies used by medicine today do work. I admit that we have many so-called scientific explanations, but I have no doubt that over the next hundred years, these explanations will be abandoned and scorned as being crude and totally inappropriate. I sometimes wonder if we know very much about any of these mechanisms. Until we do, I suggest we must look with open eyes and active minds at all healing claims, for what was yesterday's heresy may well become tomorrow's orthodoxy.

Over many years I have heard the occasional complaint about Sister Theresa's work with schizophrenic patients. My reply has been that perhaps her detractors may be right. But if I were to send 100 schizophrenic patients to Sister Theresa and 100 to any orthodox psychiatrist, I am convinced that, in the long run, her patients would be better off, especially if the measure of success is recovery and not the bare ability to sit at home, tranquillised, watching television.

A HOFFER, MD, PhD

1

A Clean Sweep for a Start

I fled Him, down the nights and down the days,
I fled Him, down the arches of the years;
I fled Him, down the labyrinthine ways
Of my own mind; and in the midst of tears
I hid from Him, and under running laughter,
Up vistaed hopes I sped;
And shot, precipitated,
Adown Titanic glooms of chasmed fears,
From those strong Feet that followed, followed after
But with unhurrying chase,
And unperturbed pace,
Deliberate, speed, majestic instancy,
They beat – and a Voice beat,
More instant than the Feet –
'All things betray thee, who betrayest Me.'

FRANCIS THOMPSON

You are in search of wholeness. So am I. I have a body, a mind, a spiritual life. You are like me in this. If my findings are of any help to you, I gladly share them. If not, may your own journey be replete with vibrant life, pressed down and overflowing.

Over the years, I learned that my spirit could not soar if my feet were heavy. My mind was confused when my blood was stagnant. To Dr Hoffer, for teaching me to care properly for my 'temple', I owe a world of thanks. To those, then, who enlarged my world with loving acceptance, in order that I might come to know and accept myself, I give heartfelt thanks. They have touched the life in me and I have grown.

The following pages begin with the earthy – the fundamental cleansing of the bowel and river system in the body. To cleanse, to build, to enhance, to come to full bloom – that is the pattern of these pages.

Experience has shown us helpful tools: diet, supplements, herbs, magnets, light, acupuncture. Then, choices of thinking patterns that pull the weeds from the garden of our souls. Finally, the crucifixion – by which we come to Easter. Only through pain do we come to wisdom. . . it is auto-learning. The transforming meditation brings these pages to conclusion.

I write chiefly from experience, that of my own recovery and as witness to the recovery of hundreds. In the latter chapters of 'coming closer to Heaven on Earth' I rely on the teachings rained upon me by significant 'Wise Men' of the late twentieth century! Their dialectic has led me to seek truth and follow after it. 'I have been searching for it all my life and now I have found it.'

This book is written at the request of a man who said exactly the same thing to me when he learned things great and wonderful, as he sat with me in session with a dozen other people who chose to *take time to grow*. It is to this I invite you, too, if you so choose. The Hound of Heaven is with us!

You come to me with a heavy heart and a body burdened. I am happy to receive you because I carry hope for you – for I have been where you are. You may speak a lot or you may simply come without words. Your eyes speak well. In either case, I listen. I consider first the physical aspects. Later, a harmony of the whole. Your own and your doctor's diagnoses are important to me.

Long ago Leo Schafer taught me a fundamental truth: ninety-nine percent of illness is stored in the *bowel*.[1]

The colon is a storage bin, a muscular tube divided into

four sections: ascending colon extending upward on the right, transverse colon which crosses the cavity to the other side, descending colon which passes down the left side, and the sigmoid colon leading to the rectum – in all, about five feet long. Peristaltic movements, contraction and relaxation of strong muscles, force the body wastes to expulsion.

Before food reaches the colon, it must journey through the small bowel, about twenty feet long. It is here that most absorption of nutrients takes place. Digestive juices are at work. The intestinal juices, the enzymes from liver and pancreas, complete the digestion of foods. If the bowels, large and small, are filled with waste materials, if the walls are coated, the person suffers a lack of absorption of water and minerals. Harmful bacteria multiply and change the colon from an elimination system to a septic tank.

To properly cleanse, it is good to add fibre to the diet. Fibre is part of all plant cells. Another name for it is cellulose, of no nutritional value and indigestible. It simply becomes water-swelled and gives body to the stool to facilitate a clean sweep of the bowel. Besides helping to cleanse the colon, it slows down the absorption of sugars and fats. A lack of fibre causes the stool to be hard and dry. This, in turn, can cause a multitude of problems: torn colons, piles, diverticulitis, appendicitis, hernia, even varicose veins.[2]

My first-hand experience showed how well the body can manage time-adjustment (jet-lag) if the bowels are cleansed. Prior to departure flight, I juice-fasted for one day. On board our flight, again only tomato juice and liquids (no alcohol!). The result was that I felt only three attacks of jet-lag, of one hour duration each, on three separate occasions in the space of one week, following a transcontinental flight. Friends of mine on the same flight, have spent a few days in bed to recuperate! My explanation is, in large part, the empty bowel. My experience was enlightening to me. It is true that many people may have difficulty trying to duplicate it. Perhaps for them it is not good.

I shall always remember a priceless tip, 'If we eat three

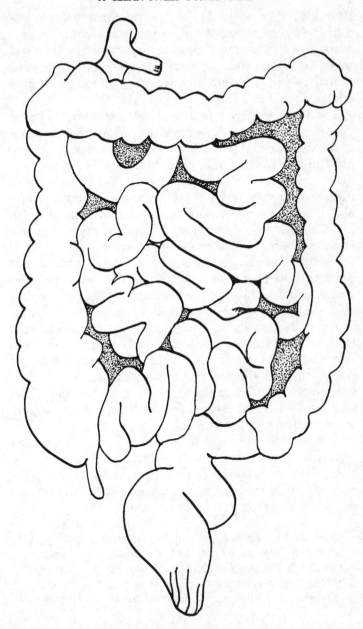

times a day, is it not well to remove the garbage three times a day?' If poisons are stored, they are absorbed. Today, I encourage two to three bowel movements daily for maximum health. (A total of eighteen inches in length, dark brown colour, and one inch in diameter for an average adult).

The *Vascular Cleanse* is increasingly necessary today. A young businessman walked into my office a few days ago, evidently in danger of his life. Elimination had become difficult, infrequent. Eating brought nausea. The eyes were a deep, toxic yellow. Eight years of search had brought multi-diagnoses, ranging from 'It will pass; it's nothing to worry about,' to ALS (amyotrophic lateral sclerosis), the dreaded Lou Gehrig's disease. He was frequently dizzy and experienced a fatigue and stiffness that alarmed him. When I listened to his story, I suspected the flow of blood was practically nil. His pallor reflected this. He drank a preparation of red Cayenne pepper, one-quarter teaspoon in a bit of cold water. This was followed with a few shots of acupuncture from a magnetic acupuncture device. The blockage in the vascular system seemed to reduce. The man's colour was returning into his cheeks... all within minutes! He visited the washroom. 'I really feel good,' were his words as he re-entered the office. Two days later, he informed me, 'I'm a new man.' He went back to work. Recent confirmation gives me to understand that he is still well.

At this point we do well to focus for a moment on the red pepper (Cayenne) as a priceless herb for the cleansing of the body. Even tar in the lungs of smokers is dislodged by the oral intake of red pepper, approximately two to three percent per one-quarter teaspoon of red pepper.

Uses: The all-supporting, stimulating effect of Capsicum (red pepper) is the infallible action of internal success. Capsicum taken with Burdock, Golden Seal, Ginger, Slippery Elm, etc., will soon diffuse itself throughout the whole system, equalising the circulation in all diseases that depend upon an

increase of blood, and unlike most of the stimu
thy, it is not narcotic.

It acts mainly upon the circulation, giving i
tion to the heart and then extending to the capil
tone to the circulation without increased pu
giving equalised power to it.[3]

A couple, well advanced into their sixties, suffered from a
medically diagnosed arthritis. They decided to try the red
pepper. Within minutes, they marvelled at the new flexibil-
ity of legs and knees, the relief of having no pressure in the
head. Both had walked with severe difficulty prior to this.

It would seem that frequently it is vascular blockage that
underlies the constipation factor, or the hernia problem or
the varicose veins. Recently, a young woman, who was
ready to start hormones 'to normalise the pituitary', found
that a drink of red pepper regularised the functions of her
uterus. It had become dysfunctional and troublesome, especially as regards the menstrual cycle. I explained to her that
my image was: 'when the blood no longer freely flows, every
organ of the body is deprived of necessary life. . . the one that
is "your weakest link" is really only the first to start telling
you about the real problem. The irregular menstrual cycle
here is but a symptom of the large problem.' I compare
frequently the garden hose. If it is plugged with clay, it
cannot be a channel of life-giving water for the garden. I was
taught to take one-quarter teaspoon of red pepper in one-
quarter cup of water, to drink this, then chase it with a glass
of cold water. Many of my visitors take it daily for two to
three weeks, then weekly. There are delicate constitutions
that find a smaller amount is more acceptable. They may use
it daily on their food, in soup, for example. Those who
maintain they cannot take any red pepper find effective
substitutes in wormwood tea or the golden seal tablets.
Similar purpose is accomplished. So it is with the vascular
system. The clay or 'blockage' needs to be dissolved. Red
pepper, wormwood, golden seal. . . marvellous herbs! True,
they may not be a panacea for all malfunctioning glands!

ɔtones, too, in gallbladder and kidney, can be problems. Blockage is common. The father of a six-year-old explained to me that after each meal the little fellow became extremely nauseated and brought up all that he had eaten. He would do this regularly in order to feel comfortable between meals. It became apparent that the lad carried blockage in the gall-bladder area, possibly stones. With about thirty shots of the acupuncture tool there were quick results. The piezo, in this case an electro-acupuncture [i.e. no needles], is the size of a big pen and is easily manipulated by an adult thumb. Two days later, the father phoned to tell me there were no more sessions of vomiting. The family was grateful.

Kidney stones evidently are removed by the same method of acupuncture. I find the following map of the body invaluable. (See lower right palm for stones.)

Sometimes the liver needs cleansing. There is evidence that chaparral strains out the poison of chemicals stored in the liver. Chaparral is an Indian term for a non-toxic desert plant of which leaves and stem are medicinal. There are claims that several cups of tea daily or a dosage of several tablets per hour are useful for toxic conditions: alcohol poisoning, boils, arthritis, acne, to mention a few. The herb chaparral cleanses deeply into muscles and tissue walls, acting as an antioxidant, antiseptic, and natural antibiotic.

The vegetable diet is itself a form of cleansing. The Hippocrates School of Nutrition recommends the meal be fifty percent raw vegetable! A juice fast is undertaken periodically, perhaps weekly or monthly, according to individual need. Doctor's supervision is desirable.

Echinacea, a herb, has been shown to be useful in cleansing the lymphatics. The lymphatic system might be compared to a drainage complex of a physical department.

These are the major areas demanding cleansing. Vascular cleanse, bowel purge, clearing of blockage in gallbladder area – this is a usual sequence of progression along the road to better health. The stomach frequently proves to be normal at once if the blockages are removed. Before this, the symp-

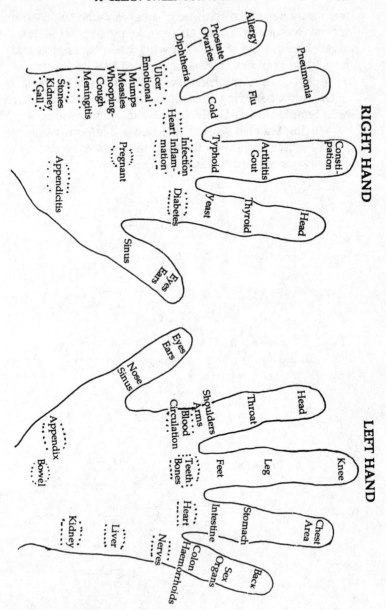

RIGHT HAND

Allergy
Prostate
Ovaries
Diphtheria
Ulcer
Emotional
Mumps
Measles
Whooping-
Cough
Meningitis
Stones
Kidney
Gall

Pneumonia
Flu
Cold
Typhoid
Arthritis
Gout
Consti-
pation

Infection
Heart Inflam-
mation
Pregnant
Diabetes
Yeast
Thyroid
Head

Appendicitis

Sinus
Eyes
Ears

LEFT HAND

Eyes
Ears
Nose
Sinus

Shoulders
Arms
Blood
Circulation
Throat
Head

Teeth
Bones
Feet
Leg
Knee

Appendix
Bowel

Heart
Intestine
Stomach
Chest
Area

Kidney
Liver
Nerves
Colon
Haemorrhoids
Sex
Organs
Back

toms may be similar to those of a person who suffers from ulcers. Doctors have been able to take patients off their tagamet! Because the blood is flowing freely again, the body goes to work in its glorious capacity to heal itself.

'I heal no one,' my friend says. 'The body heals itself.'

Given proper living conditions, the body maintains itself as 'a temple cleansed,' functional, happy and whole.

'We don't catch diseases,' says Bernard Jensen. 'We create them by breaking down the natural defences according to the way we eat, drink, think and live.'[4]

2

You Are Magnetic

The earth is a magnet. So is the sun. So is the body of everyone on the face of the earth. So is the moon, the stars, each one a magnet.

In ancient history, half a century before Christ, it is said that Queen Cleopatra used to wear a magnet on her forehead to appear ever youthful. A Swiss alchemist and physician already in the sixteenth century pioneered work on the magnet, according to Dr H. L. Bansal and Dr R. S. Bansal of India.[5] It is the work of these two doctors in their book, *Magnetic Cure For Common Diseases*, that has opened my eyes to the fantastic gift of magnetism. I draw heavily from the work of these two doctors, who confirmed for me what I have been discovering about the power of the magnet: MAGNETISM IS ONE OF THE BASIC PRINCIPLES UNDERLYING ALL EXISTENCE.

Sir Dr Leo Schafer, of Saskatchewan, Canada, had introduced me to the power of a magnet in 1977. Already then I had glimpses of magnetised water having a strength beyond that of ordinary water.

A number of years ago, I had placed a magnet for twenty minutes over my nasal cavities, in the hope of improving the situation of a cold. The magnet I used was too strong for the face. For three days I was scarcely able to open my eyes. The experience left no doubt in my mind that the magnet had a power far beyond my understanding. Then I read the book, *BioMagnetism*, by Albert Roy Davis.[6] I came to understand that magnetism is basically a process of re-alignment of ions, molecules if you like, both of which and all of which are themselves magnets, with a distinct polarity, north or south, needing a magnet to align them, in order to become a second magnet.

Childhood studies of magnetic fields gave me to understand that there was indeed some truth to the fact that a storm at sea or excessive sun could affect my body. I learned that the Hindu calendar and many ancient civilisation calendars were set according to the moon. Biblical reference is replete with examples of the same (*Numbers* 28: 11).

From experience I have learned that sleeping with one's head to the north is one way of allowing magnetic energy to flow through the body such-wise that sleep is peaceful, even dreamless. Apparently among the Hindus a person who is dying is placed sometimes in this position in order to pass on with the least possible difficulty.[7]

This is allied, I believe, with my own certainty that earth and mud are powerful magnets for healing pain. Many a time I used to watch the farm dog put his nose into wet mud after receiving a dozen quills from the porcupine. I watched the pigs on the farm. If one of them had a sore portion of his anatomy, the cool and comforting burial in the mud brought relief. I believe I would make an excellent citizen of India! I love earth!

Listen to the exposé of the human magnet by Drs Bansal:

> Man is a tiny replica of the vast universe and possesses similar elements and qualities. As the innumerable planets in the vast universe are balanced and kept in their orbits by magnetism, so the human structure is sustained by the same force.[8]

In summary, magnetic therapy means simply that we balance the magnetic field within the body. What a marvellous tool is the magnetic earth! What a delicate instrument is the human body, and what treasures we have in high power magnets, mountains, and rocks and streams!

The following story is about a friend. Adele is a delight to me, exemplifying what I have just written on the topic of magnetic energy. She writes:

After frequent visits to a neurologist, I was diagnosed on 3 February 1987, as having multiple sclerosis. I had most of the symptoms: fatigue, blurred vision, pains in my arms and legs, a tingling sensation in my body – mainly in my legs, a heavy feeling in my limbs and depression. I was told that nothing much could be done.

'Just wait and see how it progresses. You might eventually have to look into a disability pension,' I was told.

I felt that no one understood how I felt. Many people said that I looked well but I thought, if they only knew how my body feels, the tiredness, the pain, and the tingling. I found it difficult to work. The symptoms of MS are worst in hot weather. By the end of the day my tingling legs felt heavy and sore. The doctor said that all he could suggest at this time was that I get a lot of rest.

I heard about the Morris Center from some friends and made an appointment to see Sister Theresa. I began a wholesome diet – no junk food, no gluten or dairy foods. I placed South Pole magnets on my thighs, knees, and calves daily for about a half-hour. I was also taking many vitamins and minerals. Every day seemed like a struggle to keep going.

On 5 September 1987, when I woke up I had no sight in my left eye. The evening before I had felt very tired and my eyes were sore and tearing, but I thought that I would feel better in the morning after a good sleep. I was terrified! A friend took me to emergency in the hospital. After many tests, the doctor put me on Prednisone (60 mg. a day) which I was to take for two weeks, decreasing the dosage during the last week. This, as a nurse, I feared to take. I was given an eye patch for my left eye. I was not to return to work until the sight returned. At times the pain in my left eye was severe. It felt as if someone were trying to pull my eye out. It became hot and tearing.

Theresa put me on carrot juice for four days, gave me more vitamins and TLC (tender, loving care). More struggle but, with the help and encouragement of all my friends, I made it. My sight returned to almost normal in January, 1988, and I returned to work.

I still had to go to the Morris Center after work to get magnet therapy for my legs. Climbing hills or walking long distances was difficult for me. My legs still felt heavy and sore.

On 17 September, 1988, I had the great opportunity to visit Lourdes. On our first day there, after a two hour wait, we got to the baths. During the wait my legs felt like painful stumps. After the bath my legs felt good – not heavy, no tingling. I could hardly believe it – A MAGNETIC MIRACLE! After the bath, my legs were functioning at six hundred and fifty times their original capacity. (Theresa's, by comparison, were at eleven hundred.)

More energy came to me by touching the rocks. The rock was one and one-half times as strong as the water. Our energy increased: mine to 755, Theresa's to 1,300.

We thought that once we got to Lourdes I would need a wheelchair to get around, but that was not the case! I kept up with the others, climbing the hills and walking about all day.

At this time, my legs still feel stronger than they did before our trip to Lourdes. They still have to be strengthened periodically by magnets and acupuncture.

There are days I still feel very tired, but I've discovered I can renew my Lourdes boost within minutes. I keep my diet and listen to my body, refuelling it with Lourdes energy. Theresa calls me her magnetic friend.

Another amazing energy available to us as often as we call it to consciousness is the power of a blessing (or a prayer). At a convention one day, the gentleman on my right was doing his best to quieten the crying child in his arms. I had just finished my address to the audience and had spoken of this blessing power. The father's struggles led me to desire deeply that the child might settle into peacefulness, so I blessed the child, touching him as lightly as I was able. The crying stopped instantly. 'Magic touch,' said a priest on my left. 'No,' I said. 'I blessed him.'

My secretary, Mabel, once set out on a twenty-seven hour bus trip to visit her children in Wisconsin. She had contracted a cold; I sincerely wished she would remain at home. Her determination to go was unshakeable. I took her to the bus depot, promising to send prayer and energy with her.

Throughout her travel, at least seven or eight times between work moments, I consciously applied magnetic energy and light to myself for her. Near midnight, immediately after her trip, I telephoned her.

'I could feel the energy all the way,' she said. 'I have no sign of a cold and I am in excellent health.'

Since that experience both of us do long-distance caring for family members and friends. My father's recent back injury, reported to me by phone, was an occasion for this. I used both acupuncture and magnets: about thirty shots of the latter tool on the tip of the little finger of my left hand (spine) and South Pole magnets (a belt) about my waist for two hours. I then muscle-tested him on myself, phoned my mother and found his condition considerably improved. . . as it is to this day!

It was another observation that prayer does the same thing for people. Many times I have seen loving parents pray for the sick child and the blockage tests less because of the prayer. Prayer is an energy. It is a force that unblocks. Love is that same energy. It melts away the blockage that makes a body sick. That is why sick people often respond to prayer and loving with a renewed physical strength, even instant healing. That is why it is so necessary that we love one another, especially sick people. All of us are doctors. I believe this is what Jesus meant when he asked us to love one another. Prayer and love and energy are the same thing.

Consider anew the reason for the Grace before each meal. We are being called to AWARENESS. Prayer is truly a conscious act.

It is, I believe, this consciousness that will revitalise and renew our lives. It is this deep listening to the vibrant energy in and around us that will reconsecrate the earth, and fill us with respect for all things created. This is the poverty of spirit – a respect for all things created – that gives the earth as inheritance. The miracle lies not in any *one* human being, but in Universal Energy that surrounds us. The danger is that, like the poet, I may miss the miracle, 'God was in me and I knew it not!'

Truth is magnetic. It comes to life within us. We give it space.

Practical Tips for Use of Magnets[9]

The recommended magnet is 1,200 to 3,200 gauss.
The *North Pole* side *kills pain and/or poison*.
The *South Pole* side *strengthens*. It is these two principles that make the magnet a priceless tool for many people who take up the task of cleansing and building.

- N-Pole passed over a plate of food in a S to N direction seven times at least, detoxifies the food.

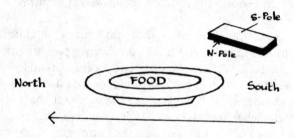

- An ordinary glass of water that is set on the N-Pole for at least seven minutes is detoxified.

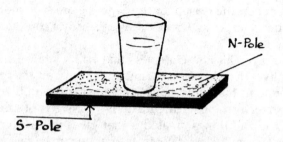

- N-Pole on navel detoxifies bowel – 30 minutes approximately.

● N-Pole on area of pain relieves, usually within minutes; i.e. a burn, a bruise.

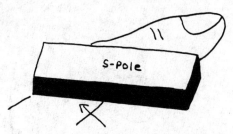

N-Pole side on burn until relief is felt.

● See drawing above, but use S-Pole to strengthen if bone has been cracked or broken (after bone has been set in place). This can be done for several days, perhaps 30 minutes daily.

● S-Pole boosts strength of organs, limbs; i.e. heart – in one minute. (*NOT used with pace-makers.*)
To boost legs – 30 minutes approximately.
(Applications can be made through the hand. See acupuncture chart on page 19.)

● S-Pole is not used for cancer, ordinarily.

● After magnetic treatment, S-Pole is touched to right palm of person receiving therapy to normalise polarity, should regular pattern have been disturbed.

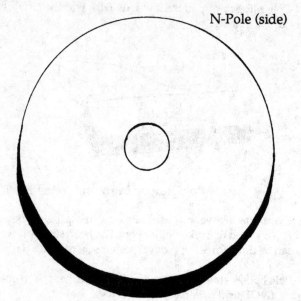

N-Pole (side)

S-Pole (underside)

(Actual size of magnet commonly used by auto suppliers.
Stronger than magnet pictured below.)

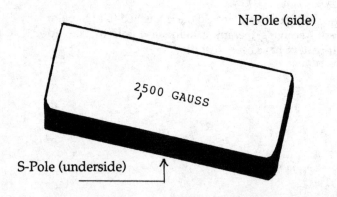

N-Pole (side)

2,500 GAUSS

S-Pole (underside)

(Actual size of one of the magnets supplied by Schafer's
Health Store, Box 251, Unity, SK, Canada, S0K 4L0.)

3

Enlightenment

I listened to a tape by John Main recently. He described the experience of ultimate energy as the experience of Jesus! Jesus said, 'I am the Light' (*John* 8: 12).

We speak of the sun as the source of all light. It is a magnet larger than our own planet. In fact, the magnetic field of the sun is considered to be one hundred times greater than that of the earth. It is the light of the sun that gives the earth day and night, the seasons, light, shade, vegetation, all types of light, fire, heat, perhaps even magnetism. Without the sun there would be no life. The sun is constantly influencing the earth. When there is a change in the sun's magnetic field, magnetic storms arise unexpectedly. There are those who believe that living creatures are also affected by these modifications of the magnetic field of the sun.

About four years ago, our Home purchased for the first time a microchip Biotone light therapy machine. It was after two years of investigations that we finally made the decision to invest in a light machine. Our hesitation was due to the fact that we needed to be certain the side-effects were good. There was much investigation, careful observation, and finally, a decision. We had discovered a tool that was indeed life-awakening to the human body. The function of the light machine, according to Dr Spiros Lenis who introduced this vehicle into our lives, is simply: 'to stimulate enzymes to restore natural function'.[10] It is the nature of light to kill harmful bacteria. The same nature of light will foster growth in the green plant. This is insight: the light has the innate power to kill the harmful and nourish the good.

The light machine depicts the seven colours of the rainbow, each of which has a unique function. The red, for example, is an activator. The yellow purifies. The blue calms. It is used for the eyes. The green light boosts the heart. The infra-red is the most penetrating of all the lights. It does an effective job of destroying harmful yeast, toxins, pain. The orange light, like a jackhammer, dissipates blockages. Every light can be used on a continuous or pulsating beam. The continuous beam sedates: the pulse activates. These are generalities, of course, about the specific lights.

Apparently, the monochromatic light stimulates the production of collagen and elastin, thus improving cellular function. LED's (light emitting diodes) have the same biological effect on the cells. Experiments done in Budapest by Professor Mester are indicative of this.

Another point is worthy of note:

The Difference Between LED and Laser Light:

Laser light is a coherent beam that has been produced in a canister with high voltage power, and helium transfer through a vibrotic wire to a hand probe. The wave-length of this light is 660 nanometres and most of the helium neon lights have an output of 2 mw.

The same light can be produced by CO_2 and argon lasers, which can exceed many thousands of milowatts. The helium neon canister has a life span from 3,000 to 5,000 hours and then has to be replaced. A helium neon light has been proven dangerous to the eye. The LED life expectancy is from 50,000 to 80,000 hours, and all that is needed to be replaced is the light emitting diode. According to the studies, the LED is not dangerous to the eye. Also, the LED, is more powerful than 2 mw and can range from 2 to 10 mw. Another advantage of the LED is that you can select a probe of different wavelengths for different colours. Therefore, you can have a whole spectrum of LIGHT on the same unit inexpensively.[11]

The Biotone model of the light machine is an irradiating, non-coherent beam, contrary to the laser which has a coherent beam, capable of cutting and burning.[12] Many a time I have watched with my own eyes the irradiation of the LED. I have seen dark red, angry sores change to a healthy pink, soft-healing flesh.

To watch the light at work is a powerful convincer. One day I burned my arm. The accident was typical. It sent me scurrying to the office where I immediately applied the light. It took probably ten seconds before the sting was gone. I marvelled; the light had stimulated the enzymes to restore natural function. Many a time my people have testified that the pain went out of their limbs in similar manner as we put the light on the body.

I teach a five day session for those who wish to learn the techniques of light therapy in conjunction with the nutritional approach. For those in possession of a light machine, I outline the following hints: (*Light Dynamics*, Lenis Ventures, is my main guide.)

- *Cranial Adjustment*: 1 minute of continuous red light on the third eye.
- *Spine Strength*: 10 minutes of pulsating red light on the tip of little finger of left hand.
- *Hip Strength*: 10 minutes of pulsing red light on side of palm, mid-point between little finger and wrist.
- *To Stop Smoking*: Place red, continuous light on right brain (1 inch above eyebrow). Give the order: 'Right brain, let go of all desire for nicotine.' Repeat this (with light) on the left brain, adding reasons: i.e., 'Left brain, let go of all desire for nicotine because X has chosen to eliminate all toxins from the body, etc.' Then place the light on the third eye to affirm: 'X, your brain has received the message. Be free of desire for nicotine.' (This method can be adapted to stop use of alcohol, overeating, or to foster recall of studies prior to exams, etc.)
- *To Detoxify Food*: Swing red continuous light in clockwise circles over food about seven to eight times. (When the light is applied to the teeth, this relieves allergy to

metal in teeth as well.)

- *Candida Albicans* (Yeast Infection): Place infra-red light, continuous beam over navel for approximately 20 minutes. (If using red light, 30 minutes may be required.)
- *Nasal Blockage*: Red continuous beam on sinuses for 5 to 10 minutes.
- *Heart Boost*: Green, pulsating light 3 to 5 minutes over heart or at base of ring finger on either hand.
- *Gallstones*: Orange, pulsating light over the gallbladder from 10 to 30 minutes, depending on the severity of blockage.
- *Laxatives*: Yellow light, continuous beam, on a glass of water for seven minutes makes the water a purgative.
- *Aching Eyes*: Blue continuous light for three minutes on each eye.

The acupuncture chart found on page 19 (two hands) will serve as an aid, as will the reflexology map of the body (hands and feet). The therapist keeps in mind that the pulsating light strengthens, whereas the continuous beam sedates. The therapist's intuition will be an invaluable guide as the path of the toxins in the body is discovered and the remedial tools applied in the interests of life and wholeness. An image of tissues mending, of blood again given freedom to flow, of nutrients carried to a scene of deprivation – all this visualisation allows maximum energy exchange through the body of the therapist and the receiver. It becomes a gift given. The joy capitulates when the gift is received and a person is renewed.

'I am the Light of of the world; the Light of Life' (*John* 8: 12).

Two case histories
Recently, a sister-friend came with arm in cast. She had fallen on ice. Eight weeks were scheduled for her to wear the cast. She received a thirty minute treatment, through the hands, with the red pulsating light. At home, Margaret continued treatment with a magnet, using the south pole.

At the six week check-up, the doctor remarked that the limb had already healed so well that the cast would not need to be replaced. The arm was ready for its 'maiden voyage' without support.

In January 1988, a young man and his wife came. The man had been diagnosed as a cancer patient. The chest cavity had about nine cups of superfluous fluid, I estimated. Five people worked. My helpers administered red pepper for arterial and vein cleansing. Light and magnets boosted every possible area of his body, often through the hand, especially on the local trouble scene (chest). Within the hour, the man felt relief. In two days, when I saw him again, he was noticeably improved. The fluid was definitely draining. The body was gaining strength. Life was flowing with increasing vigour.

In September 1988, eight months later, I met him again at Lourdes for a second bath! He was now employed, feeling well, still baffling the doctors, who had no explanation for his recovery.

4

Building My Cathedral

*God made the human body, and it is by far the most exquisite and
wonderful organisation which has come to us from the Divine
Hand.*

H. W. BEECHER

I love the stones of Ireland. Sister Concilio, one day, gave me
a rosary of Connemara marble. Each bead bespeaks solidity.
Every rock, every stone wall, every enduring castle, even the
timeless ruins of the monasteries remind me that the chain is
as strong as its weakest link.

So it is with my body. I have many processes at work in my
body. If any one of them fails, I suffer breakdown (as does the
car when the ignition fails).

Within my body is a digestive system. It may be that my
teeth are broken, that my stomach juices are lacking enzymes, that I am missing amino acids or co-enzymes. I may
even be missing the space in which my stomach best functions (perhaps the gallstones are blocking the space the
stomach needs). Perhaps my digestive juices are not flowing
for reasons physical or metaphysical. It is a known fact that
fear can so inhibit the digestive juices that food eaten at
mealtime lies unassimilated hours later. Hence the advice
not to eat when we are disturbed. Much better it is to subsist
on juices which nourish the body and, at the same time, do
not demand labour on the part of the digestive system until
the emotions are calm and the digestive juices are flowing
again.

There is a vascular system in the body. If this becomes plugged, it is as the garden hose plugged with clay, dirt or stone. How then can the irrigating waters, the life-giving waters flow through and inspire the withering flowers to raise their heads? The vascular system is easily unplugged. Red pepper is excellent for some people. One-quarter teaspoon in a few ounces of water may relieve high blood pressure. I have seen instant relief for many people who were suffering from this problem. A glass of water is taken after the pepper. If the red pepper is too unpleasant, there is the vitamin, inositol, an effective cleanser. Of course, there are more sophisticated ways of cleaning the vascular system, one of which is chelation therapy.

This treatment is more costly, but it does relieve. The chelation process is one in which the blockage of the arteries is reversed or reduced. It involves the injection of a synthetic amino acid (EDTA) into the blood stream. The resulting interaction on minerals in the plaque causes them to become bound and carried to the kidneys for normal elimination. The plaque then releases surplus cholesterol and other substances as well, since its cementing ingredient (calcium) is dislodged. Cholesterol travels to the liver, where most of it will be used in the production of bile. This method of cleansing is effective within weeks.

The wonders of red pepper need to be known. I am delighted that one pastor in Manitoba had the courage to publish in the back of his bulletin the marvels of red pepper, or Cayenne, as it is commonly called. Would that every pastor were so conscious of his temple that he might make known to his sheep one of the simplest ways of preserving happiness in the body. The need is monstrous! Many doctors know the value of red pepper.

The elimination system is part of our bodies. We so easily shy away from speaking about it. It is earthy. Without fail I emphasise that in my classes. I quote what Sir Dr Leo Schafer taught me because it rings beautifully true: ninety-nine percent of our illness is stored in the bowel! Again the famous

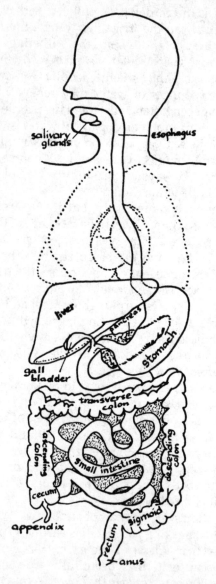

The alimentary canal and related structures.

or infamous bottom line: 'If we eat three times a day we need to eliminate three times a day; otherwise we are storing poison.' Again, Leo Schafer says we need to eliminate approximately eighteen inches daily, a stool that is a healthy dark brown, a good inch or more in diameter. When the faeces is finger thick, one-half inch in diameter, no doubt the walls of the bowel are heavily coated with faecal matter that must necessarily be removed if we are to live in the hope of not beginning disease in the walls of the bowel. It is surely in the aged, decayed matter of the bowel that poisons are born and stored and soaked up into the body osmotically through the veins.

There is a respiratory system in the body. It stores our precious supply of oxygen and fresh air, breath and life.

Nicotine, on the other hand, is the chief evil threatening the destruction of our respiratory equipment. Of course the drug is not the problem, rather only a symptom of a greater, underlying need. Society says it is okay behaviour to be puffing away at a cigarette, even though practically every one of the smokers realises that the habit is harmful, deadly. Smokers often are aware of the dangers of the warning printed on the package of cigarettes. That is, intellectually they are aware. But do they see deeply?

Nicotine Deadly

Nicotine is a poison so lethal that if you were to swallow the amount extracted from five cigarettes, you would die within three minutes. Inhaled nicotine blocks certain nerve action, constricts small blood vessels, and interferes with the liver's ability to dispose of fats after a meal.

(from *The Healthy Heart*, Arthur Fisher, *Time Life Books*)[13]

Vitamin C will remove some tar, red pepper will remove some tar, south pole of magnet will strengthen the lungs, acupuncture will open energy highways, time will allow the body to heal itself. All these things, all these measures may be taken for the lungs to be restored.

Recently, an elderly gentleman came with his family and

oxygen tank. The oxygen had been used for over a year. The gentleman drank red pepper in water three times (¼ teaspoon pepper with each glass of water), and for the better part of an hour he spewed out mucus. I asked him then how he felt.

'Much better,' he said. For about six months, this man no longer needed his tank. When winter arrived, he used it again.

Today, he is happier, remarkably improved, bringing family and friends to adopt the red pepper drink. In addition, he has brought other elderly people from the neighbourhood in which he resides because he has become aware that he has the capacity to rebuild his cathedral even at the age of ripe maturity. Rebuild the cathedral and enjoy precious more breath in praise of Him who gave the cathedral in the first place. Again I am grateful for the witness of this man, for the gratitude he lives for the breath of life.

Sometimes the glandular system has relapsed into slow gear in our bodies, or high gear for that matter. Multiglandulars, raw glandulars are excellent to strengthen, to stimulate natural activity. Worthy of notice is a raw bovine substance called Ovarian Substance for ladies. This and the herb black cohosh become priceless at the time of menopause. Within days they bring relief from the hot flushes consistently experienced. For few people there is need to look further for relief from the discomforts of menopause. The HER Nucleoprotein and the HIS Nucleoprotein are multiglandulars. They are particularly useful when pituitary, thyroid and adrenal glands are functioning abnormally. They are no panacea, of course.

The structural system of the body is the most instantaneously rewarding! At times, knees that are weak and feet that are hurting will come to strength and solidity within minutes when the acupuncture tool, the pulsating light, or the south pole of the magnet are applied. Sometimes it is the cranium that needs adjustment. Often, one moment of the South Pole magnet is sufficient to adjust the cranium, even as it is the atlas, that part of the nape, or administration office (as my friend in Japan calls it because all messages pass through it en route from spine to brain). Then we have the hips, which are quite easily strengthened again with the pulsing light on the buttocks, or the South Pole, or the acupuncture.

There is also the reproductive system. It is effectively contacted through the tiny finger of the left hand (the middle joint). The genital organs experience relief from pain practically instantaneously with light, acupuncture or magnet. In all these processes we are rebuilding a system, renewing a strength that has been broken. In each case the basic underlying principle is this: I take away the barrier to proper functioning; the body begins again to restore itself! So I take away toxic food, the barrier of over-exertion, or negative thinking. I revise the manner in which I exert myself at work, recreation, etc. I take away the barriers of worry and the barriers of fear and anxiety. It is like pulling away the rushes in which a boat has become stuck or a barge in the river. I unhook the boat and it continues to move with the current. Even so our body continues to mend itself if we take away the barriers to good health.

'You are an amazing person,' I am frequently told. 'Yes,' I reply,'but if you wish, I will teach you, too, how you can do these amazing things, because it is *not in me* that the amazement lies, but rather in the *wonder of my temple*, my body, how it functions, how it heals itself, given proper environment. I am only, like John, "a voice in the wilderness." Some see, and some walk away sad. There is a choice.'

Everyone who comes to me asks me the question, 'How do I get my answers?' That is an important question. Most people need to know how the statistics are achieved, the percentages, the conclusions. For this reason I speak aloud or half audibly, if the person wishes. I explain kinesiology, the muscle test. It is a test used in the ancient world for centuries. It is not magic. It is a simple science. For some people it becomes an art. The test is basically a measurement of the current of energy in the body.

Dr Lenis has this to say about muscle testing in his textbook *Light Dynamics*:

> After the basic work was done and Applied Kinesiology was established by Dr Goodheart, Dr Thie and others, many people found that it could be used as a means to receive messages from the body. They found that when you asked the body a question which can be answered 'yes' or 'no', the muscles would become strong or weak. It was established that a strong muscle test was the response for 'yes' and weak for 'no'. Within a few years many versions of Applied Kinesiology were being taught with various trade names: Touch for Health, Biokinesiology, Kinesionics, Integrated Structural Therapy, Orthobionomy, etc. Each one is an expansion of the basic idea of Applied Kinesiology in a direction approved by the persons involved.[14]

Of course, it is important to know that the muscle test is not a god. It is only a guide. It is, however, a good guide. Advantages are many: a) in a few seconds we are able to discover information about the body: b) the test is inexpensive: c) there is no harmful radiation absorbed by the body: d) we retest on the spot if there is any doubt about the validity of the answer.

Application of the Muscle Test

- Face client toward the north, about 6 inches to the right of the therapist. Test the arm for strength. The therapist's palm is cupped on the wrist. Note the client's wrist is partially flexed.
- The client says: 'I am Tom.' If this is true, the arm tests strong. If not, the arm tests weak.
- The therapist makes the statement: i.e., 'Tom is able to eat wheat.' Strong indicates 'yes'; weak indicates 'no'.

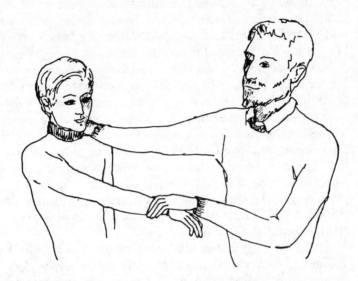

There are a few factors we need to consider when we look at validity. It is important that we avoid, for example, the following:

- sitting or standing under direct light
- exposure to electrical outlets
- standing in front of radio, telephone or television
- standing on the earth's meridians – this is why we recommend that we face the person who is being tested in the north or south direction
- if we are testing a food, we place that food in the hand or mouth for the test, and do not confuse the test by having other foods nearby
- we avoid exposure to many colours
- we advise there be no distracting persons in the room, be they family members, children, or even a voice from a tape recorder
- we do not test when the person is under emotional stress and is having difficulty thinking about what is happening
- we remove all jewellery, metal, eye-glasses
- we recommend that the therapist be consciously aware of clearing himself/herself from any distractions

Personally, I have found the muscle test a sensitive tool, an exquisite gift on the part of our Maker. It helps me to understand the intricacies, the delicateness of the human body, such that it takes the breath away.

I remember when I was still in regular classrooms, teaching the subject 'health' to grade seven and eight students. In the public school text there was a simple picture of the earth with a string tied three and a half times around the perimeter. Below the picture was the shocking information that if the veins, arteries and capillaries of the vascular system of the human body were tied end to end, we would have a string long enough to go three and a half times around the perimeter of the earth. When I consider this, I cannot but marvel at the wonder of who I am, the wonder of who you are, the wonder of Our Maker!

'I thank you for the wonder of my being' (*Psalm* 138:14).

The diet, my daily sustenance, my supplements, food supplements (called vitamins and minerals), sometimes a few herbs (particularly herbal tea), all of these are the Connemara marble for the priceless cathedral for which I have the blueprint! It is my responsibility to repair my cathedral. I have had others helping me in the building of this cathedral, but the repair jobs are *my* responsibility. Albert Schweitzer puts it beautifully. I use his words to describe my responsibility as I become doctor to myself: 'The true doctor simply awakens the physician within to achieve ultimate health for the patient's mind and body.'[15]

It took me a long time to learn personal responsibility for my body. In 1970 I became ill, hopelessly sad with a problem in my body. Four medical doctors diagnosed schizophrenia. I was given medication and my misery doubled. For over a year I struggled with the decision to seek more help and more help and more help, simply because I was no longer able to cope without help. Life was quickly becoming impossible. After four months in the hands of an expert on the other side of the American continent, I returned home heavily medicated, most unhappy, unable to visualise how I could endure even tomorrow, not to mention a future.

As the days went by it became more and more clear to me that suicide was the only answer. I saw no other. I had tried friends. Family could not understand. Counsellors advised routes that were closed to me, impossible routes. 'Sing,' one told me. How could I sing when I could not sing? In any case suicide was the only answer. It was in the depths of dire need that I was referred to Dr Abram Hoffer, in Saskatoon.

Dr Hoffer was the internationally known biochemist who, in 1952, had discovered that megavitamin therapy is effective in the treatment of schizophrenia. Incidentally I had not heard of his work before. He spoke with me for approximately three minutes and said, 'Sister, we will pump you full of niacin and watch what happens.'

Vitamin B3 and a diet! No more sugar, caffeine or white flour. This was my program for nineteen days. I awakened on 27 November with a brand new experience of life. My depression had lifted! I felt like bouncing out of bed...I felt like going to school for the first time in a couple of years. I could scarcely contain my joy. I wanted to share that I was feeling like a different person.

As time went on I learned that the niacin (B3) had soaked up the adrenalutin, a toxin in my body. About thirteen years later I learned still more, that the niacin had cleared the cholesterol out of my vascular system, allowing the blood to flow again. A retrospective kinesiology test revealed that my arteries and veins had been ninety-five percent blocked at the peak of my illness. Now I understood the extreme fatigue, the dizzy spells, the memory loss, the sluggishness. My elimination system had slowed down to the point where I was dependent on laxatives. Sickness had caused radical change. I had wondered if I was possessed. Existence had become morbid.

Interestingly enough, my craving for milk had led me to consume five to six cups daily. Plenty of sugar daily had been my diet. Today, I recognise both milk and sugar as dangerous for my health. I do not touch either one. In my convent home where the kitchen supplied food for over a hundred people, I had easily fed my addictions: sugar, caffeine, white flour pastry, macaroni, milk, catsup, ice-cream! My need was to be re-educated.

After nineteen days of megavitamin therapy, my misery came to an end. I sensed new life in my body. This new life intensified for the next six months, 'till I wondered if I might explode with it, so strong was the surge of energy. My being was alive, vibrant. I felt like singing.

Five years later, when I was already back in regular class-room teaching, questions began to rise within me. Why had I become ill? What was the cause?

I was already helping a lot of people to choose the same route I had chosen with their diets and supplements. (I knew little else in terms of helping sick people.) The diet and Vitamin B3 alone brought many people back to health. (Vitamin B3 in Canada is found under the name of niacin, or niacinamide. In Ireland, the product is nicotinamide.) The tablets recommended are 500 mg. strength. Often two to six tablets are required. Dr Allan Cott reports in *Doctors speak on the Orthomolecular approach*:

> . . . *The dosage recommended by them is 3 – 9 grams per day*, as determined by the response of the patient, of either Nicotinic Acid or Nicotinamide, together with Ascorbic acid and other vitamins.
>
> Nicotinic Acid and Nicotinamide are non-toxic. The lethal dose is not known for humans, but *it is over 200 grams*. Their side-effects, even in continued massive doses are not serious and subside quickly with the reduction of the dose. The most common side-effect to nicotinamide is nausea. Niacin produces a flushing and reddening of the skin which subsides in about one hour and does not usually recur after the fifth or sixth dose.
>
> Among the advantages of Nicotinic Acid are the following: *it is safe, inexpensive, and easy to administer*; it can be taken for years with only small probability of unfavourable side-effects.

After experiencing great success in the treatment of schizophrenic adults with Vitamins B_3, B_6, C, and others, I applied the treatment to children suffering from childhood schizophrenia. I found the improvement in many children to be more dramatic than in adults. I then began to investigate the possibility of extending the treatment to the other psychoses of childhood, principally autism. I hypothesised that autism was, like schizophrenia, the result of a metabolic disorder and that the overlapping symptoms of the two illnesses were manifestations of the perceptual distortions which resulted from the presence of toxic substances in the bloodstream and of the improper molecular concentration of certain vital vitamin and enzyme substances in the cells of the brain.

Schizophrenic and autistic children have many of their senses altered. The world of these children is not at all like ours. They may suffer distortions in the perception of time, space, depth, vision, hearing, and of their own bodies. . .[16]

5

Eat What is Set before You

It was the then National Director of the Canadian Schizo-phrenia Foundation, Irwin Kahan, who said to me that we are in greater danger of destroying ourselves through mal-nutrition than by nuclear warfare.

One day after Hallowe'en – my first three phone calls were:

'Could you see my boy? He's so hyper. . . !'

'Could you see Cyndy before school? The teacher says she never sits still anymore.'

'I'd love to bring my children this week. They really need it.'

Many teachers see what junk food is doing to children's behaviour. Some of them testify:

'I know it's coffee that keeps me awake.'

'One chocolate bar is too much. I get a splitting headache.'

'I used to live on cake. Now it makes me sick.'

It used to be a virtue to 'eat what is set before you.' Today, I call it a great virtue (strength) to turn away from the sugared dainties, the doughnuts, the fluffy pastries that characterise social functions. I have friends who would never touch the sweetmeats they bring to the church base-ment to raise money for the poor. They would be ill if they ate their own offerings!

In today's language we could find a new translation for 'Eat what is set before you': Take responsibility for what you set on your table. When the body has reached its capacity for junk food (sugar, caffeine, white flour), it signals in any

number of ways:
- immediate body discomfort, vexation, stuffiness
- headache, sharp or dull
- constipation – overstorage of toxins
- indigestion or flatulence
- sudden sleepiness, a heavy foot on the gas pedal
- non-connectedness in mind and thinking
- tension – at the steering wheel or elsewhere
- impatience, a tendency to blame others

I tell people every day I have no right to break my health programme. I tell people frequently the day is coming when a Catholic confession will consist of something similar to the following: 'Bless me, Father, because I have again eaten the chocolate bars that make me inoperable at the wheel. I have again drunk the milk that makes me incapable of doing an honest day's work. Bless me, Father, because in that blessing you touch life in me that I have chosen to drain from my body, my temple, a choice I have made to pull out the foundation blocks of my temple. A choice I have made to decrease the time and the energy with which to serve You. A choice I have made to slice from my body so many years of life during which time I might glorify my Maker.' This I see as at least one aspect of the new morality.

The issue that, of course, lies behind this morality is that of responsibility. As recently as October, 1988, I was on board a jet-liner returning from Toronto. My friend and I were served lasagna, dark yellow cheese, a white fluffy bun, cracker, wine, coffee, milk and a dessert pudding. Even one part of that meal would have made me uncomfortable. If I had taken the whole of it, I would have arrived home very ill. As it was, I chose to drink only juices on flight and came home that evening in good health, ready for work the following day.

I see about a dozen people a day. Certainly at least eleven out of twelve of them share my dependence on proper diet. How can I then teach that it is okay to eat whatever is set before me, that it is okay for someone to eat junk food, that it is okay to have cake and ice-cream for dessert – that is, the kind of cake and ice-cream that is loaded with sugar, white flour, chemicals? How can I say that it is okay for people to continue enjoying junk food and not instead teach the life-giving truth of caring for my temple in a way that becomes it?

Already sixteen years ago health was restored to my body by means of eliminating sugar, caffeine and white flour from my diet. (I didn't know about milk at that time; I was drinking milk but I wasn't aware that it was indeed an allergy for me.) Already then I felt within me such a need to share this good news that it was humanly impossible not to say it aloud. To my surprise I found that many people could not hear it. It was too much. It implied change, painful change. To hear the word would be to act upon the word. A readiness was missing. I recognise today that this readiness is no longer missing.

It is possible for me to break my diet in order to escape responsibility. I may choose to smoke and drink in order to remain 'cared for'. This is the behaviour of a child. I remember my own temptation to stay sick sixteen years ago. The label had been given me: schizophrenia (a label denies my truth – there was more to me than my sickness). I had been told that I would need medication forever. I had been la-belled one who would never be independent of doctor care. This would have been insupportable slavery. But even in the midst of this slavery I counted the benefits of never needing to go to work again. I brooded over the temptation of never needing to check eighty compositions weekly in the school where I would have otherwise been teaching. I pondered never needing again to be responsible for decisions, for duties, even for prayer. I could play the child now. I had a reason. I was 'mentally' ill. I could receive letters by the dozen from those who were doing charity. I could receive roses as one who is ill and needs to be cheered. I could receive condescending visits from authorities, visits that I would never get at home if I were on my feet. All this I remember so well. The temptation to give in and to hug the slavery of my schizophrenic imprisonment! It was strong.

Today I have grown. The 'physician within' has been awakened, as Albert Schweitzer says. I take responsibility for eating what is good for me and take the responsibility for setting that dish before myself. It might be the herbal tea, or the distilled water, or the magnetised food, or the organic carob bar, or the organic vegetable pie. It is my responsibility to make sure that what is set before me is REAL FOOD, food that is 'alive as possible (i.e. sprouts), whole as possible, non-toxic and varied.'[17]

If this is true for me, is the situation otherwise for the rest of humankind? For those who wish to refine their dining experiences and to reap a harvest of tranquillity of body, and serenity of mind, I suggest the following:

Possibilities for Breakfast: My best recommendation is the grapefruit breakfast. Quite easily one can make a meal out of a grapefruit plus one other fruit, excepting the banana. The banana may be eaten as a snack later on in the day, but for breakfast when the body is undergoing a cycle of elimination, we suggest the acid and the subacid fruit. Besides the grapefruit there is a choice of the orange, lemon, pineapple, the sour plum, pomegranite, strawberries. There are also the subacid fruits – apples, apricots, cherries, grapes, mangoes, papaya, or the pear. The avocado could be eaten at breakfast or in the afternoon as a snack.

The body's morning cycle is one of elimination. Generally speaking, this morning cycle consists of the time from 4:00 am until noon. It is followed by the intake cycle from noon until 8:00 pm; then the absorption cycle from 8:00 pm until 4:00 am, according to the book, *Fit For Life*, with which many of you are familiar.[18] I have found it personally rewarding to embrace this cyclical eating pattern.

The Noon Meal could consist of protein such as nuts, whole grains, dried beans, peas, olives. If meat is taken, poultry or fish might be served, a white cheese at times (not coloured), or sea foods. In addition, the green salad is complementary.

The greens assume importance as a source of calcium, since we do not recommend milk.

Milk is dangerous for several reasons. It has mucous-producing characteristics, as do other dairy products. It is 'high in fat' which makes it a major dietary culprit. Milk ranks high in the cause of allergies, the symptoms of which include 'gastrointestinal problems', 'respiratory reactions', 'behavioural changes', blood and skin deficiencies. Hodgkins disease is a cancer, the development of which is implicated with dairy food. Sudden infant death syndrome (SIDS) has been linked with milk allergy. Most people cannot digest milk properly. Milk does more harm than good for ulcers.[19] The addition of chemical preservatives to milk and milk cartons further endangers our milk supply.

The Evening Meal then is the starch meal The potato, white or red, the yam, the squash is in order. Whole grains might be used, since they are both a starch and a protein. Likewise, dried beans, peas, pumpkin, artichokes, carrots and beets. The salad again is desirable, as well as lightly steamed greens.

Snacks throughout the day consist of nuts, seeds, fruit. Perhaps a celery stick with peanut butter on it! Perhaps a whole grain peanut butter sandwich! Or a tomato!

Melons are peculiar. According to the Hippocrates School of Nutrition: 'Eat them alone or leave them alone'.

Chemicals remain a problem for the body. Whether they are sprayed on the vegetables or injected into a vein, our bodies do not 'naturalise' this foreign invader. Increasing numbers of people are requiring organic food in order to escape the chemical plague.

Eventually we will come to see what is happening. Our dependence on the aspirin bottle, on emergency instant pain relief reflects our running from the responsibility of dealing with our pain. This constant running keeps us infantile. We do not grow by running from the problem. We miss the rewards of listening to a marvellous teacher, pain (see p. 77).

To conclude, a few case histories of people for whom a

select diet is a privilege. It makes a difference what they eat.

The first story deals with a four-year-old boy, who came to our home in the arms of a desperate mother. A doctor had told her it would be best to 'institutionalise the child and try to forget that he is yours.' Within twenty-four hours the child betrayed his addiction. He was at the table with the family. I can still see his little arm reaching half way across the huge family table to grasp with his fingers, the peanut butter bowl. When it came within twelve inches of his plate, both hands shot out to grasp the bowl and bring it quickly to his face, without the use of any spoon or fork. He simply poured the contents into his face in a desire to eat as much as possible, as fast as possible, the peanut butter that he craved. Thus, his intuitive mother discovered his allergy to peanuts, to wheat, to whole grain bread, to sugar, to chocolate, to milk. If I remember correctly, this little boy was brought every day to our home, to eat at our house.

Within days his mother saw a tremendous difference. He was receiving a bread made from non-gluten flour, namely buckwheat and millet. He was touching no milk and no sugar, no chocolate (caffeine). Several years after his departure from our home, I received a photograph in the mail. There was the same little boy making the headlines for a shop. They were using him to advertise the Father's Day sales. He looked as healthy, and strong and beautiful as any lad I have seen. A personal photograph of a boy seven years of age was also in the envelope, with a 'Thank You', to our home, for the new life received. A more recent contact with his mother leaves me assured that the lad is still doing well. He is today a young man with opportunity and every possibility of success. He is confined to a limited diet, in Canada. If he were to live in Europe, there would be a greater choice.

Anne – I shall call her 'miracle Anne'. The miracle lay in the fact that this lady, at seventy-five years, did not give up. She arrived on 17 December, 1987. Weight: 175 lbs (about 12.5 stone). Her complaints were high blood pressure and arthritis. She used a cane. With the assistance of her husband, she managed to place herself upon my table. She was taking three medications, including a blood thinner and prednisone. Her eyes did not focus properly. Her history included eighteen strokes, surgeries for gallbladder, hysterectomy, tonsils. She had a goiter problem and had previously had jaundice. Her legs were swollen at least twice normal size. She had gallbladder problems. She could not sleep for pain.

Anne took the bowel cleanse with cascara, then did a colon-cleansing kit (a preparation of bentonite clay and psyllium seed), both major steps. The acupuncture and magnets were used to cleanse gallbladder and liver. Capsicum and garlic were daily fare. She ate vegetables, chicken and fish, millet and fruit. She took vitamin B6, B5, a multivitamin-mineral, co-enzyme Q-10, White Oak Bark for pain. One year later, Anne has no pain, no drugs, good eyes, and legs practically normal. The neighbours are asking her how she did it! Many are learning from her experience.

I first saw Bill in September, 1986. He was seventy-three years old. Bill had a condition diagnosed as cancer of the blood. He was functioning painfully, at a level of approximately sixty-five percent. It was easy to see that he was full of harmful yeast and totally toxic. Bill was constipated. He had gallbladder trouble. His vascular system seemed severely blocked. We found Bill to be allergic to gluten products and dairy products, that is, he became more ill by eating wheat, oats, barley, rye, corn, rice (except the wild rice), milk and cheese. He indicated that his liver was functioning poorly. Initially, Bill decided that he would take herbs to cleanse the bowel, the herb chaparral for the liver, red pepper or Cayenne to cleanse the blood. For three weeks, his breakfast diet was one grapefruit. In addition, Bill needed to do some building of his body. He was taking two multivitamin-minerals, cod liver oil, and Taheebo Tea. Propolis, a natural antibiotic made by the bees, is another supplement that Bill was using. (Natural supplements are preferable to the synthetic.)

When I saw Bill again, he was considerably better. In fact, he was bringing to me family members and others of his acquaintance. On his last visit, which was in October 1988, approximately two years after our first meeting, I found Bill so hardy and healthy, I would have liked to put him on the front page of a newspaper, with the headline, 'How to Live When You Have Been Pronounced Dead'.

Today, Bill's diet has become much broader. He still loves the fruit breakfast, whether it be grapefruit, kiwi, pineapple, peaches, pears, berries of the season, or almost any fruit. Bananas are too sweet for him. Whole grains are permitted, even pumpernickel bread; organic grains are the specialty.

All vegetables are welcomed on his platter, but no red meats. Chicken and fish are allowed. These proteins are eaten separately from potatoes and other heavy starches.

Bill rarely touches cheese. Tofu is a substitute. The only dairy product for Bill is a bit of butter. He drinks tomato juice, herbal tea or herbal coffee. As for cheating, though he's not scrupulous about his food, I know he will remain faithful to a junk-free, allergy-free diet as long as his body enjoys life.

I also know you can scarcely meet a happier man! Or a happier wife! How well they have learned to be selective about every dish that is placed upon the family table.

And God said, Behold, I have given you every herb bearing seed, which is upon the face of all the earth, and every tree, in which is the fruit of a tree yielding seed; to you it shall be for meat (*Genesis* 1: 29).

. . . and the fruit thereof shall be for meat, and the leaf thereof for medicine (*Ezekiel* 47: 12).

6

Healthy and Whole

Good health is inexhaustible richness; the benefits are beyond measure. Without health, life can be difficult. Ill health usually means toxin in the body. Sometimes, a few tips can help restore health in remarkably simple ways. They are not meant to replace your family doctor. They are to be used for education, not the practice of medicine.

● **Headaches**

Ask the question: Why?

1) Constipation? a herb, i.e. Stomach Ease or Herbal Vita Lax, can help.

2) Allergy? a magnet, i.e. place north pole side on inside of either thumb.

3) Stress? Massage, i.e. neck area or webs of hands.

● **Constipation** is the major cause of headaches. Plenty of fibre in the diet, raw vegetables, oat bran, adequate liquid (6-7 glasses daily), these counteract a problem of constipation.

More persistent problems may call for Senna or Cascara, for colonics, or the Colovada Kit for colon-cleansing. Radical cleansing is done with the co-operation of your doctor.

● **Vascular Blockage** causes problems of every kind.

1) An excellent remedy is ¼ teaspoon red pepper, taken daily in water for 2 weeks (adults only).

2) Inositol, a B vitamin: 250 mg. twice daily for a month is effective.

3) Oral chelation: Ora Key and Ultimate, 2 to 4 tablets daily for one to two months.

The arteries and veins are comparable to a garden hose. If

it is clogged, the waters cannot irrigate the garden. Blood pressure is significantly lowered when blood vessels are cleansed.

● **Gallbladder blockages** are common and painful.

1) One vegetarian day, one vegetable juice day, then 6 doses of olive oil (2 oz. each) taken 15 minutes apart and chased by 2 tbsp. of freshly squeezed lemon juice. (Begin, for example, at 7:00 pm of the day on juices.) Next day stones pass with bowel movements.

2) A recipe of 3 heads (bells) of garlic, 3 grapefruit and 3 lemons. Peel them, blend them (blender), eat them as a meal or two, twice weekly for 2 to 3 weeks. Even large stones disappear.

● **The Common Cold** – Sinus – Hay Fever

1) The red pepper ($^1/_4$ teaspoon taken daily in water for 2 weeks), is effective. Never used with children, of course, though the parent is able to take the drink for the child when holding the child's hand or even thinking lovingly of the child.

2) Propolis (a natural antibiotic, made by bees). 2 to 10 daily.

3) Vitamin C: 10 to 50 grams daily, or to point of diarrhoea.

4) Magnet: North Pole on lowest third of ring finger of right hand over night.

5) Acupuncture: 30 shots on lower third of ring finger of right hand. (Electro-Acupuncture without needles.)

6) The recipe of 3 heads (balls) of garlic, 3 grapefruit and 3 lemons is most effective for colds, and easy to take! Peel them, blend them (blender), eat them as a meal or two, twice weekly for 2 to 3 weeks.

7) Plenty of sleep.

● **Obesity**

1) Eliminate sugar, caffeine, white flour and processed milk from the diet.

2) Exercise reasonably.

3) A quarter of a teaspoon of red pepper, taken daily in water for 2 weeks is important for the blood to flow freely (adults only).

4) Guar Gest: 2 tablets per meal for adults. (Amni product).

● **Smoking**: 'Nicotine is a poison so lethal that if you were to swallow the amount extracted from five cigarettes, you would die within three minutes.'[20]

1) Visualisation: see yourself with the benefits of non-smokers.

2) A quarter of a teaspoon of red pepper, taken daily in water for 2 weeks is of utmost importance for basic strength of body (adults only).

3) Vitamin C: 3 to 10 grams daily, Folic Acid 400 to 800 mcg. three times daily to preserve lungs.[21]

4) Acupuncture: visit a natural therapist for this.

● **Squinting Eyes**

1) Check your need for cod liver oil.

2) A quarter of a teaspoon of red pepper, taken daily in water for 2 weeks for basic health (adults only).

● **Insomnia**

Ask the question: Why?

1) Junk food? Eliminate sugar, caffeine, white flour, and processed milk.

2) Stress? Niacinamide (500 mg.) (natural). Dose varies from 3 to 6 grams daily depending on age, weight or length of illness; lesser doses may also be used, of course.[22]

3) Colour Therapy: calm colours are pale blue, green, mauve. Avoid red, pink, yellow and dark colours.

4) Position of bed: head to the north allows for natural restoration of energy due to earth meridians.

5) Food: only a light snack (if any) two hours before bed-time.

6) Sleepy Time herbs: Camomile, Valerian, Hops, combination Five, Cloud Nine. (2 to 4 tablets an hour before retiring.)

● **Broken Bones**

The South Pole of a magnet reduces healing time. Small magnets can be applied to arms, legs and kept in position at least 30 minutes twice daily or all night.

● **Food Detoxification**

A plate at the restaurant, for example, may contain a dangerous ingredient such as sugar. The North Pole of the magnet is passed over the plate (2 inches above it) from South to North seven times. The dinner is likely to cause no discomfort.

● **Water Purifier**

The use of the magnet as in 'Food Detoxification' is equally effective in purifying a glass of water. An alternative method is that of placing your glass of water on the North Pole side of the magnet for seven minutes.

● **Lower Back Pain**

1) Use South Pole of magnet over kidneys or on lower right corner of left palm for thirty minutes twice daily. *This technique is not used when cancer is present in the body*.

2) Acupuncture on tip of smallest finger of left hand will maximise energy flow to the spine. (20 to 30 shots – adults only.)

● **Asthma**

1) A quarter of a teaspoon of red pepper, taken daily in water for 2 weeks is excellent (adults only).

2) Acupuncture on tips of ring fingers of both hands (20 shots) maximises energy flow to the lungs.

3) North Pole first, then South Pole of magnet is placed on tips of ring fingers of both hands, each 30 minutes, twice daily.

4) Junk free diet: eliminate sugar, caffeine, white flour, processed milk, and often the gluten grains (wheat, oats, barley, rye, corn, rice). Yeast, of course, is avoided.

● **Food Combining**

For maximum digestion comfort, minimum flatulence:

1) Eat fruit outside the meal, an hour before or two hours after.

2) Drink liquids 20 minutes before the meal.

3) Never eat meat and starchy vegetables, such as potatoes, together (protein and starch do not mix well). Noon meal: protein and greens; Evening meal: starch and greens.

● **Menstrual Cramps**

Vitamin B6, Iron, Zinc, A & D, E.

● **Warts**

Garlic oil, rubbed into wart nightly for several weeks will often result in the disappearance of the wart.

● **Ulcers**

A quarter of a teaspoon of red pepper, taken daily in water for 2 weeks, contrary to expectations, works marvels for ulcers (adults only).

● **Skin Disorder**

1) Vitamins A & D for dry skin.

2) Zinc to neutralise toxicity, i.e. mercury or aluminium.

3) Vitamin E for nervous system. A herb sarsaparilla.

● **Haemorrhoids**

1) Sitting on the North Pole of the magnet brings quick relief.

2) See 'Constipation', the underlying cause of haemorrhoids.

● **Hair Loss**

1) Inositol, a B vitamin, especially in young people is often the answer.

2) Vitamins A & D, E, Folic Acid.

● **Diabetes**

1) Elimination of sugar, caffeine, white flour and processed milk.

2) The herbal Combination Eight, 4 tablets daily (Pure Life product.).

● **Hypoglycemia**

1) Elimination of sugar, caffeine, white flour, processed milk from diet. Basic Food Programme consists of Vegetables, Chicken, Fish, Nuts, Seeds, Whole Grains, herbal liquids.

2) It is essential that some nourishment be taken at least every three hours to provide glucose for the brain.

● **Arthritis**

1) Elimination of sugar, caffeine, white flour, processed milk from the diet.

2) Gluten products often need to be eliminated also (wheat, oats, barley, rye, corn, white and brown rice) as well as yeast.

3) A recipe of 3 heads (bells) of garlic, 3 grapefruit and 3 lemons is excellent to detoxify the body. Peel them, blend them (blender), eat them as a meal or two, twice weekly for 2 to 3 weeks.

4) Niacinamide (500 mg.) three to six grams daily are frequently needed.

● **Depression**

1) Vitamin B3 (niacin or niacinamide) 500 mg. tablet, 3 to 6. (The time-release product may cause a problem. Your doctor may caution about side-effect of flushing, generally harmless.)

2) Zinc, the anti-depressant mineral.

● **Yeast**

1) Plenty of garlic

2) A quarter of a teaspoon of red pepper, taken daily in water for 2 weeks (adults only).

3) North Pole of magnet over navel each night for several nights.

4) Elimination of sugar, caffeine, white flour, milk, cheese, yeast, mushrooms, vinegar, dried fruits, grapes and plums from the diet.

5) Yeast-Aid, a kit for a one-month therapy (Pure Life product).

The above are tips, not completed therapeutical programmes for distress of body and mind. It is recommended that having read this book, you discuss your problem with your doctor, then choose your course of action.

Central to all remedy is the practice of gathering one's energies daily (or twice daily) in periods of silence and meditation.

● **Effects of Drugs**

Drug identification through web analysis. A young Swiss pharmacologist discovered that spiders will spin erratic webs when doped with drugs. Different drugs affect different parts of the nervous system and cause the spiders to produce a characteristic web pattern for each type of drug.[23]

When a man is dead, he has a brain with all centres

presumably remaining intact. Yet there is no life in him. The brain does not function, because the soul has departed. The soul exists before we are born, and the faculties are there. They cannot, however, function in the world of matter except through the brain. Body and brain are the soul's media of manifestation in the world of matter. At night, when brain and body are wrapped in slumber, the soul can depart from the body and can function on its own through dreams. Anesthetics drive the soul from the body, allowing us to cut, burn and slash the body, brain and nerves, as we please, without the soul's knowledge. But when the soul returns, so does consciousness, body awareness and the sensation of pain.[24]

EFFECTS OF DRUGS

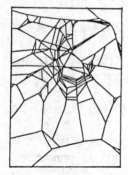

CAFFEINE

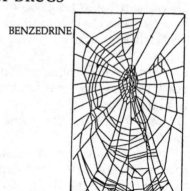

BENZEDRINE

NORMAL

7

Second Healing

The marvel of the physical transformation was sufficient to pre-occupy me for five years. It was then, with increasing frequency, that questions came to mind. Was diet the only factor that contributed to my illness? What was the meaning of the deep search within me? How could I explain my feelings? What connection was there between my history and my illness? I still had many answers to find. . . my search for meaning was not yet clear to me.

One day I met a lady who touched me. Her name was Doreen. She had done a weekend growth session at our convent and spoke of self-image, of dealing with negative and positive forces within us. I recall being provoked at losing precious time for my follow-up work with my English classes. At the break, Doreen stood near me, put her hand on my shoulder and spoke to me. I do not remember our sharing, but in that instant my disposition changed. My anger melted. I went to my seat with an attitude of listening and learning.

Doreen became a surrogate mother for about ten years. I shall always love her. She seemed the first person to see a needy child in me, a child who needed to grow. Her kindness, gentleness and wisdom completely fascinated me. I listened to every word she spoke. I became her disciple. One of the tools she placed in my hands was PRH (Personality and Human Relations). Any adult who wishes to travel the road of personal growth is able to do so more easily with the help of a PRH session. The movement was begun in France in 1970 by André Rochais, a man whose deep call in life was to provide the tool of growth that would facilitate the development of the human personality – unto fullness of capacity.

In time I came to know the reason for my anger, my fears, my pain. I was able to talk about it, cry about it, write about it, share it, and grow strong. Today I have a body that is physically sound, a mind that is a wonderful servant to the core of my being, a spirit that is daily nourished with love and truth. I am a new creation, no longer a slave of untruth. My growth continues. 'The physician within' has been awakened. I am grateful for the gift of life and the responsibility of re-building my cathedral.

Re-building is a process which frequently involves a demolition of the old, prior to solid construction of the new. Some of my demolition involved a radical screening of my belief system. I found there the old die-hards of lethal power:

- my happiness depends on the degree of perfection I am able to attain as an individual dedicated to hard work and sparse leisure. (It was in PRH sessions that I came to understand the tragedy that necessarily follows from this belief.)

- it is my duty to keep others happy – at any cost. I was a responsible person only if I succeeded! (Small wonder that I struggled with continuous disappointment. There was always someone who was miserable! It was always my fault!)

- without the approval of others, I am worth nothing. (Today I have heard the Gospel [Good News]. The Kingdom is within. It has nothing to do with the approval of others. I have always been priceless. I was made that way. God makes no junk.)

- God is angry with me when I behave in undesirable manner. (God is not the victim of my choice of action; I am.)

Once the new bricks of a solid belief system came into my line of vision, I sensed a joy within that nothing can ever take away from me. It is the experience of having touched the infinity that lives within me. I shall never die. The essence of my being will live forever. 'I, too, must be eternal like you' (*Psalm* 138:18).

8

The Best is Free

E. J. Pratt (1882–1964), in one of his poems, explains how the sea traced granite features into a cliff. Then he contrasts nature (the sea) placing, in the space of one hour, 'the sculpture of these granite seams upon a woman's face'. The Canadian Pratt understood something of the power of nature. In a moment of pressure, one hour of intense art, the sea achieved the work of a thousand years.

Many people are affected by water. It touches the life within us. It may lead us to relive the anguish that is buried deeply inside or it may loose to sudden freedom a gift that was formerly in chains. All nature has this power, this capacity to touch us, to awaken us, to bring us to a stirring.

A tree may touch wonder in us. I remember the power awakened in me when I read a poem by Amoral Kent. It spoke of a tree in a gale, swaying, bending, almost breaking. It spoke of the storm lashing, whipping, almost overpowering. The last lines say everything:

And in that moment there passed into me
The courage to go on through my own storm.

My being grows stronger as I stand rapt in nature. I may churn with a slashing storm or experience my capacity for infinity as I measure myself against a mountain! My capacity for infinity lies deep within my being. In this core of me, there is nothing negative. It is in-dwelt with goodness and beauty, and gentleness and compassion. When I live from my being, it is impossible to act out of darkness, or despair, or doubt.

When nature touches the pain in me, awakens the hurt of past history, I need to remember that feelings are not destructive; actions can be. My actions become destructive only when I condemn or reject my feelings. In themselves, feelings are neither good nor bad. They simply are.

The gift lies in awareness of my pain. Nature effectively teaches awareness. Once I become acquainted with my feelings, I can deal with them. If I avoid my hurtful feelings and don't identify them as part of me, or even if I am aware of them, but battle them, they become ugly. To battle with my feelings is to condemn myself for having them. The condemned part of me gets nasty (feels judged)! *Awareness*, deep, full awareness makes my energy outflow more positive.

The step following awareness is *acknowledgement*. If the ocean has touched me with its moaning, I become aware of the sobbing in my body. I am then in a position to see my own response, or acknowledge it. The ocean has been a gift. I receive it as such. 'A gift is not a gift unless it is received.' It may be that the contents of my feelings are far from beautiful (anger, fear, pain), but when I share these contents *as my truth*, I am always beautiful. Having shared, I can the more easily accept that *all this* is ME. Acceptance is the stage of peace! An African proverb: Once I accept my limp, I begin to dance! Or, a second morsel of wisdom: Unless I accept my faults, I will most certainly doubt my virtues! The reward of all this is that once I accept my behaviour, I no longer see it as a fault. The axe has been laid to the judgment that kills!

And so it is that nature teaches. I may need to stand for hours in a forest simply listening. I may need to gape, open-mouthed at the orchestra in the sky. To watch a catfish earn his keep is a marvel in itself, or to follow a puff of breath thrown into the air as it struggles with time and disappears. From the moving river, I learn that water does not return to where it has already been. So it is with a past that cannot be relived. What is, is, even as the breath is gone. But peace has nothing to do with perfection. . . 'There is more joy in Heaven'

(*Luke* 15: 7). A child learns to walk from many times having stumbled.

As life grows stronger within me, it pushes up the pain. As water poured into a jar expels the air, so my life expels the pain. Nature causes life to stir within and to rise from a dormant state. The stages of my journey are awareness, acknowledgement and acceptance. The final stage includes acceptance of my history. When I accept all of me, I am invincible.

Nature is my mirror, a doorway to my past, and a revelation of my inner being. By the time I know myself, I will have come to know My Maker. In the process of my growth, my own consciousness is given over to full consciousness of Life and Energy, of Love and Grace, and Prayer and Truth. In that full consciousness I am one with My Maker. It is then that I am free...with the freedom revealed by Jesus. This is insight (power). Oliver Wendell Holmes said, 'A moment's insight is sometimes worth a life's experience'.

The physical benefits of exercise and rest are, likewise, to be noted. Nowhere do I find a couch more comforting than earth, nowhere a trampoline more permissive of rebound! To rest my quota, to trample my acre is a must. It is in this daily resting and rising that I discover the insight of Emerson: 'There is one direction in which *all space* is open to him (each of us).'

'I came that they may have life and have it to the full' (*John* 10: 10).

9

I Am Born Good

I marvelled as I watched the people in their wheelchairs. . . dozens of them. Perhaps you've been in hospitals or homes where you've observed many people on stretchers, in carriages, pulled by the sturdy. Perhaps you've looked at their faces and experienced gratitude for your health. In Lourdes, the wheelchairs and the stretchers have the right of way. The amazing thing about the sick, however, is the unspoken announcement: 'I am allowed to be here! I have a claim to the space here!'

This, I believe, is one root explanation of the healing that goes on at Lourdes.

'I have a right to be.' If this belief is shaken in me by my historical past, or my present experience, I am in a state of turmoil which I describe as hell! These pages are all about a journey away from hell, a journey towards life.

Numerous people come to me with a burden on their backs, a burden that is another form of crucifixion. I give you this example, a friend in a state of utter exhaustion. She sighs: 'I guess I am just no good anymore!'

'I *know* you are good. I know *others* who *know* you are good,' I say.

'But I hate my husband, I've even stolen from him, I'm hard on my kids, I don't care enough to cook the meals or clean the house! I never was any good!'

'I'm hearing that your *behaviour* is not acceptable in your own eyes, but that has nothing to do with you as a *person*!'

'What you say is true. I need to separate my behaviour and

my person. *What I am doing* is not good. But *I* am good. I was always good – even from the beginning. My behaviour is my choice.'

'Your behaviour is your choice. At times we make the choice to change our behaviour. This is a responsible act. . . to behave according to my beliefs, to make life-awakening choices.'

'The readiness is all.' When I am ready for responsible choices, I am ready to grow. Today, there is a readiness to return to basic truths. Whether the readiness is born of modern societal needs or spiritual wisdom or both will not distract me. 'Unless I am ready, there will be no teaching.' A gift is no gift unless it is received.

If I begin on the premise that I *am* good, regardless of my behaviour, I begin to live in truth. Certainly, nothing evil can come from the Hands of my Maker. In fact, there is that aspect of my being that endures. Says the psalmist: 'I, too, must be eternal like you' (*Psalm* 138: 18) as he considers the incomprehensibility of God, His thoughts, His creative acts.

John Main, in his book, *The Present Christ*, says:

The Spirit dwells in us as absolute gift, unconditionally. It dwells in us in our ordinary humanity, a humanity that is weak, vain or silly, that knows failure, mistakes, and false starts. Yet it persists within us with the complete commitment of love. It dwells within us through the humanity of Christ and it is through the mutual openness, the union of our consciousness with His that we are empowered to make that absolute response which is the secret meaning of our creation.[25]

Indeed, I am good. As for my behaviour, that may or may not be another matter.

In my lifetime, I have spoken untruth. I have loved and hated full circle those people who have blocked my path or awakened life in me. But unless I have stumbled, I do not know the experience of rising. Never to be forgotten is a day when I disclosed what to me were my most hideous, secret crimes. The response of my 'teacher', who listened more than he spoke, was simply, 'It's the best thing that ever happened to you. Now you will begin to grow!'

The gift of our *felix culpa* is the awareness it creates. No longer do I see myself as perfect! No longer do I see my Maker as One who demands perfection! I begin to recognise the truth. I see the reality: that I am indeed a privileged pilgrim, gifted with the capacity to love despite my whatever behaviour! It is not my good deeds that earn my status. . . I am loved regardless. The Creator's love is not measured out according to my behaviour. If I am given to see this reality, my choices are a loving response because 'He has first loved us'. So it is that prisons and rules become unnecessary.

What happens to me if, for some reason, I believe the lie that I am no good? I confuse my living with the demons of fear, anxiety, blame, negativity, discouragement, despair. Every devil brings seven more. I enter a state of non-life. It is a choice I make, perhaps unconscious, but nonetheless, a choice.

If I believe the lie of a label, I find myself boxed in, deprived of my capacity to touch infinity! I guarantee myself a hell for my future and exhaustion for the present. I stand in need of rescue.

It becomes imperative that I go more deeply inside – to the realm of Truth, where I know that I am good. There is more to me than my weakness. There is a denial of gift in the label. It tells untruth about me. Jensen says: 'Exalt the great within where healing really begins.'[26]

In the area of psychosexual growth, it is easy to believe the lie of being worthless, if, for example, I have had rigorously instilled into me a fear of any sexually-related behaviour. When the behaviour falls even a shade short of perfect (*perfection is impossible*), I condemn myself for having fallen in a 'so terrible' way. The usual fears are:

● fear of sin
● fear of pregnancy

● fear of disease
● fear of perversion

When these fears are fed by ignorance, by social and religious myths (*lies*), healthy growth in these areas is impossible.

A sense of humour is an advantage. The problem is that we usually lose our humour when we suffer from fears in regard to our sexuality. Fears breed more fears. We become incapable of enjoying a joke. Hence, the importance of a 'wild movie' or a 'crazy thing to do'.

I remember a visit home during the days of my melancholy. My presence among my brothers and sisters was like a wet wrap in freezing January. They conspired. We had a roll-away (a bed that folded in half and rolled). Into the V of this bed I was dropped, amid the squabble of four or five who decided that I either join the fun or go to bed. It is the one moment I loved of the entire visit – and I remember it still with gratitude. They folded up the bed until breathing was like the hiss of five geese in disharmony! Their sense of humour – an ounce of life for me!

Milton describes laughter 'holding his sides'. The release of tension is incredible, as it is when we cry! In fact, when we laugh, the life in us often achieves enough strength to push up pain. The transition is frequently a matter of seconds. What gift it is to touch our pain!

Healthy psychosexual growth includes four specific dimensions:

● A *cognitive perception* of oneself, one's body, one's gender and growth-producing sexual behaviour in a factual and positive awareness, and perceiving the body gender and the growth-producing sexual behaviour of the opposite sex with a positive attitude simply stated, a truthful exposition and acceptance of the reality and facts of our sexual and genital natures.

● An *emotional dimension* of feeling comfortable, confident and competent with one's body and sexuality and with the bodies and sexuality of the opposite sex.

● A *social dimension* of relating to the same and opposite sex in ways that are unselfconscious, open, and potentially mutually fulfilling.

● A *moral dimension* of *valuing* the ways of allowing and encouraging the behaviour necessary for ongoing sexual growth, thus preventing the harmful expression of one's sexuality.

Perhaps the most necessary understanding we can absorb is this: it is *normal* for each one of us to go through certain stages of psychosexual growth. From a state of unawareness, I need to travel to a state of sexual awakening; I pass through a time of sexual secrecy, learning that my fantasies, feelings and secret acts are a normal growth experience. Sexual fantasy is another stage of normal growth. Then a time of sexual pre-occupation, again a normal stage.

Sometimes, a superficial sexual relating is especially appealing to the person who is dependent on parental affirmation. There may be a stage of psychosexual mutuality which still bespeaks superficiality and dependency.

Finally, integration. This may happen already in young adulthood and continues until physical death. Now the entire issue finds its place among life's varied concerns. It assumes an importance in keeping with values such as career, family, friendships, growth, etc. It becomes a lovely thread in the tapestry of the whole person, a thread of natural blend, of harmonious colour and delicate perfume. It is then I easily recognise my sexuality for the great gift it is.

'I thank you for the wonder of my being' (*Psalm* 138: 14). 'You made (us) inferior only to yourself' (*Psalm* 8: 6).

Distinction: Sexuality is a gift. It refers to my masculinity or my femininity.
Genitality is a gift. It refers to my physical parts, which identify my sexuality.

10

Impurity

This chapter deals with pollution in reference to wholeness. To become whole (holy) is a simple process, but not an easy one.

To live from my being, from the qualities that dwell in my innermost, my compassion, my goodness, my gentleness, is to live in full consciousness of Ultimate Energy. It is to know Heaven on earth. I am easily distracted.

Distraction No. 1 is my inflated self-image. Whether it be that of a perfect religious or a parish messiah, my image makes demands. This trap easily leads to the exhausting syndrome of 'never good enough. . . there was one more soul I could have saved today! . . . there would have been no disturbance had I given a bit more time to so and so!' Always, there is the self-blame, the self-judgment, the self-condemnation because I was less than perfect. This is the tragedy of the impossible ideal. When eventually my self-image crashes, as it must, I am deflated. A usual pattern is discouragement, depression, sickness. The body is a delicate vehicle. The demands of perfection, the rigidity of the self-imposition, my unrealistic expectations, are forerunners of breakdown. I become a prisoner of my own image. There is no freedom. There is no life. We are called to be whole, not perfect. To be 'whole' means being comfortable with all of me.

Distraction No. 2 focuses on others and the expectations of others. To others I give the power to control my life. 'What will others think?' is the priority criterion of my actions. My choices stem from this consideration. I rob myself of the strength to act from my being, from my own life. I live in a state of dependency. (It is a childhood state.) If I become aware that this is my reality, I can begin the move toward a healthy independence (a teenage state), and eventually achieve the goal of interdependence (maturity).

Distraction No. 3 is that of my hurt feelings or very wounded sensibility. I am referring to the fear, the shame, the hurt, the anger and self-hatred that invade my life. 'Whenever you are in pain,' I can still hear one of my teachers, 'be sure you are believing a lie.' My feelings are based on my belief system. *If I believe I am no good*, I will feel a burden to myself and others. *If I believe I am rejected*, I will reject myself. (This is the most painful rejection.) *If I believe death is terrible*, I will fear death. *If I believe I am not good enough*, I can give to breaking-point and still demand more of myself. *If I believe that I am perfect*, I will repeatedly be disappointed. *If I believe my life depends on the opinions of others*, I will never have my own conscience. In each case, it is believing the lie that causes the pain.

Distraction No. 4 is that of my head, my 'I'. It refers to my ambitions, my ideas, my ideals, my rationalising, and my cerebral functioning. It is here that measurement and judgment are framed; i.e. 'It isn't fair'. The expectation is set up that all must be treated equally. It robs me of peace. Beneath the expectation lies my need to be recognised or seen, or preferred or counted. Perhaps I have difficulty taking the back seat! I want to drink from the same cup as the Apostle on the right hand. These ambitions clutter my head and block the life that needs to flow from the depth of my being. The mind stands ready for radical cleansing! The final chapter deals precisely with this.

The journey toward wholeness requires the skill of separation. This capacity to separate needs to be taught already at the level of childhood. The three-year-old smashes a new toy of his playmate. The offended child runs to his mother to spill his grief. The mother, aware that the neighbour's three-year-old is a precious child (every child is so), but that his behaviour is unacceptable, has an excellent opportunity to teach her child the art of separating person from behaviour. She says: 'Jimmy is a good boy, but I don't like what he is doing. We will have to do something about it.'

Next day the child may hear: 'You are a wonderful boy and I love you. But I do not want you playing piano with the knives and forks!'

In time the child learns. He is good. He is always good. He was born good. He is loved unconditionally. But his behaviour. . . that may need censoring.

Religion is easily used to pollute my life. A shocking example is the threat of hell. I used it well to control the behaviour of my students. 'If you disobey, you build up your own fire for hell.'

Hell is a choice of non-life. It has nothing to do with children returning to class promptly or risking overtime after school. It was a tool I used to enforce discipline. We teach as we have been taught (for the most part). Thus, as generations passed, religion became a handy tool for behaviour control, useful to compensate for insecurities and fears, erroneous in depicting the God of love and truth.

Obedient children learn a healthy discipline. I am in favour of wholesome discipline. It is the focus that may be perversive. The discipline is desirable and conducive for growth of the child. In fact, it is necessary. But the discipline is a tool for encouraging fidelity to growth. It is not meant to instil fear of eternal fire. The focus is the key.

The matter of mistakes – how often does a child stumble before it learns to walk? *Felix culpa* is exactly that! It is not so important how we learn, but that we learn. As the saying goes, 'There are many paths up the mountain, but the view from the top is the same.' Does it really matter that my history includes two years in one grade once I've graduated? Does it matter that my history includes thievery, or illegitimate pregnancy, or murder, or alcoholism, once I've hooked up my energy lines with the Ultimate Energy Source and live from my truth and my love? The past, no matter how darkened with falling, is part of my journey. It can become my doorway to wholeness. I need courage, humility, openness and perseverence. No one has ever been doomed for stumbling – only for choosing to stay in the down position. The healing is in the choice.

Guilt, fear, shame and anxiety – these are the real demons. They are not from God. They are burdens we lay on ourselves, a form of self-punishment. They are born of judgment and judgment kills. 'Judge not and you will not be judged. Do not condemn and you will not be condemned' (*Matthew* 7: 1). The injunction applies also to ourselves.

In our efforts to live from our being, it is important that we are in touch with life-giving relationships. We need people strong enough to remain standing as we deal with our anger and fears and disproportionate reactions. The strong person becomes a teacher, a discerning eye, not judging, but recognising the movement within us. The teacher has a role of calling forth the disciple or releasing the hidden splendour that is in each one of us since creation by Splendour itself!

I need to find the person I can trust. I need to talk. In time I will need to relive the pain of the past. Once this is done, the pain loses its power over me. Only a memory remains, no sting. The poison has been drained.

This process of growth takes years. In time, the disciple learns to see his own goodness, his strength. He comes to maturity and responsible choices. Activity flows from his being, rather than from the ideals of the 'I' or the woundedness of his history. There are fewer distractions. Life pushes on, gaining momentum because the disciple is in touch with Energy of infinite capacity. 'Mission Accomplished' in the sense that a ship is launched! 'Never finished' in the sense that the journey is always just beginning! Through it all we recognise that the journey of growth is never without pain. I call pain a marvellous teacher.

>   To heal
> we peel away layers to expose our
>   original pain.

> To grow
> we unfold layers and discover our
>   original being.
> Tho' not yet healed, integrated or
>   not yet our true selves
> We are like a bud growing into a rose
> the petals of what went before creating
>   the beauty of the rose today.
>   The petals of growth and pain reveal –
>   at every moment – – – – MA'–RA'–NA'–THA'!
>   the beauty of a Rose!

(ANONYMOUS)

Jensen summarises in his unique manner:

We may need a spinal adjustment to improve innervation but we also need to change our attitudes. . .
. . . By expanding our vision and opening to a new way of life, we can restore wholeness to ourselves. Quite possibly in this way, any so-called disease we have will disappear.[27]

11

Marvellous Teachers

PAIN

Dr Bernard Jensen's mother died of lung disease at thirty. His similar weakness led him into the field of health and a path to a higher way of life. 'It is through overcoming inherent weaknesses and obstacles that we develop the power and resolve to seek the higher path. These things are necessary for the development of the soul. We find that the brain is the instrument of the soul's activity and obstacles become stepping stones to a higher way.'[28]

My friend in Japan says simply, 'The person who has not suffered is worth nothing.' Only through suffering and pain do we discover meaning in our lives. We come to know what dwells in us, and discover the name is *truth* and *meaning* and *love*. The details of how we arrive at our truth or the specifics of our content are less important than how we live this! Whether my pain is via broken bones or bankrupt pocket-book is less important. What matters is how I live the pain. It is a gift if I receive it as such! It has transforming power if I allow it to disclose what lives in me, ultimately, my *truth* and my *love*.

Even on the physical level, a man shovelling his walk may experience sharp pain in his arm. If he heeds the signal, he is fortunate to avoid a total collapse. Pain was his warning, a gift. It could be tragedy to ignore such a signal.

If I confuse pain with death, I miss its benefits. Pain is an indicator for necessary change, a trouble light, an alert. What I do with that alert is my choice.

Consider the robin and the sparrow in dialogue:

Said the robin to the sparrow,
'I would really like to know
Why those busy human beings
Rush around and hurry so.'
Said the sparrow to the robin,
'I don't know but could it be
That they have no Heavenly Father
Such as cares for you and me?'

The poem teaches a basic trust. A father cares for his children. He does not promise life without pain, but 'My grace is sufficient for thee!' (2 *Corinthians* 12: 9, 10).

At random I popped the question to a dozen people, 'What has pain taught you throughout life?'

'Pain teaches me that I am not alone. Others, too, have their suffering.'

'It teaches me not to depend on others.'

'Pain has taught me to act.'

'Pain has taught me to change things.'

'I have learned to acknowledge and accept my faults.'

'I have learned to choose God's Will, not my own, to live and think positively.'

'It has taught me awareness of what lives in me.'

'Pain brings life.'

'Growth without pain is non-existent.'

'Pain has taught me my own strength.'

'I have learned that pain is reflective of only part of me. There is more to me than my pain.'

Pain is a doorway opened to me in order that I might go inside to my very depths. Humiliating memories from the past can make me afraid to listen to my inner self and feelings for fear of what I might find when I do. I fear that when I really face the truth about myself, I will know for sure that my worst fears are in fact true – that I am somehow viler than others or perhaps less 'normal' than everyone else I know. I 'run'. I run from facing my inner loneliness and am terrified of either solitude or intimacy.

I escape into intellectual rationalisation, blame (others or self), or into the defence of anger, guilt, doubt, etc., etc. But integration (healing) means the courage to acknowledge the ignoble things in my past or present. . . with the virtue of self-acceptance. My feelings never set me free. The humility of truth gives lasting freedom. In humility, I discover the richness of my being. That gives me cause for dancing. 'May your inner selves grow strong. . . ' (*Ephesians* 3: 16-19).

I walked into a church one day several months ago. The homilist held everyone rapt. I listened and recognised Goethe's lines:

> It is much easier to recognise error than to find truth, for error lies on the surface and may be overcome; but truth lies in the depths, and the search for it is not given to everyone.

It was Michael Trent, deacon and perceptive teacher who said:

> If you are committed to the truth, you must be ready to stand alone, just as Jesus did. . .
>
> . . . Truth is often challenging and difficult. Truth can often embarrass people and make them feel very uncomfortable. No wonder that people who speak the truth often end up alone. Why then do they do it? What is the use of speaking the truth if it brings such unfortunate results? Jesus assures us that the TRUTH WILL SET US FREE. . .
>
> . . . In the search for earthly power and influence, truth is always the first thing to be cast aside. It seems to get in the way. The search for truth and the search for power are totally incompatible.[29]

As disciples of Truth, we do well to search and not to count the cost, for what have we if we acquire all things and carry restless hearts? For Truth's sake, come hell or high water, like Paul, we have the capacity to endure all things. Our eyes have not seen, our ears have never heard the wonders awaiting us if we but focus on Truth. Pain then assumes its proper perspective: it becomes a stepping-stone. Did not Christ have to suffer in order to enter into His Glory (*Luke* 24: 26)?

TREASURE FOUND

Truth is found on children's lips
And seen in old men's eyes.
It dwells within the simple soul,
Sends dreams to make us wise.

It meets defences face to face
The forked tongue it kills
Cohabiting despite a storm,
The cup of joy it fills.

Then where is truth? I ask myself.
This treasure, I must seek.
I'll cross the ocean, scale the heights
And work eight days a week!

Then gently, when I close my eyes
In silence I perceive
The Truth. It dwells within my depths.
Quite slowly...I believe.

(7 December, 1989)

DREAMS

I thank the Lord Who counsels me,
Who even at night directs my heart.

(*Psalm*: 16)

If there is any moment when all of us stand defenceless before our Maker, it is in the moment of sleep. Whatever comes, comes.

– An angel spoke to Joseph: 'Do not be afraid' (*Matthew* 1: 20).
– Pharaoh told Joseph, 'In my dream I was standing on the bank of the Nile' (*Genesis* 41: 17).
– To you and me...

Dream language is unique. The dream is an encounter with Truth and Reality. It is a marvellous way to listen to God.

Dreams are as direct a speech of 'God' as any human is ever likely to encounter. The dream speaks in an archaic language (hard to recognise), which is not immediately discernible; the dream speaks in the language of symbol, of metaphor, of ceremony. If you think you know what a dream says when you first have it, be sure you are wrong, because if you understood immediately and easily what the dream is saying to you, you wouldn't have the need to dream. *A dream will never tell you anything you already know*. It won't waste its time or your time.

A dream is telling you something that you don't know.

Start all your work on dreams on that basis. The dream is giving you information which you should have and do not have. Dreams will continue to pound upon you until you 'wake up' or become aware! This accounts for repetitive dreams, or themes that keep turning up in your dreams, until you understand.

Dreams generally come in four parts:
- The person and the place concerned
- The problem
- What do you do about the problem?
- The outcome

Work to do:

a) List your associations, i.e. 'car' – freedom, power, sex; 'death' – a symbol of life.

b) The dream is an interior reality, your interior life laid out for you.

A dream will never waste as much as one word, so every detail is important. Scenery also is important. It is something of profound importance, every detail. Everything is pertinent, a cross-section of your own interior make-up, a superb way of showing YOU to you.

Dreams demand a lot of work but not as much as it seems,

because dreams are highly repetitive. If you will see one dream through and understand it, you will save yourself fifty dreams in the future!

If you work at one dream, you will need fewer. Working through an epic dream clears most of the rubbish in the unconscious areas. No one can tell you what a dream means except you. You are the translator of your dream.

A dream has to be put through four stages (this has nothing to do with the four stages of the dream).

● Make associations
● What part of me is this?
● Interpretation
● Do something about the dream

Stage 1: Associations: You can search through a person and find the 'ouch' points psychologically. These are the wounded complexes that one dreams about.

A complex is a perfectly normal, psychic development which we all contain. A complex in the sense of illness means that some 'wiring' went wrong and when one is touched in one area, something quite irrationally goes off in another area.

The dream will tell you what to do. No dream leaves you hanging with a problem. There is always a hint as to what to do.

Stage 2: What part of me is this? Interiorise the dream. Inside my own make-up is the part the dream is telling me about; i.e. my false perceptions. I dream about a complex inside myself. The complex is a circle of energy in me. When have I recently seen this part of me? If I touch a complex and draw it forth, I will get a flow of energy in my being. So it means going through the whole dream again. This means more ink and paper. (A complex is a focal point of psychic energy around a particular subject.)

Stage 3: Interpretation: What is the dream for? Why the dream? What is being accomplished in me? What do I need to learn? What is it warning me about? What is it goading me to do or stop doing?

Stage 4: Here you do something about the dream or in honour of the dream. One must go with one's physical body and do some tangible thing in honour of the dream. Celebrate the dream with your body.

There is no teacher for wisdom. Each one learns wisdom by oneself. The dream is given that the hidden splendour of each one may be revealed.

Those who take their dreams seriously often find that they are led into a deeper understanding of the spiritual world. As they bring the dreams before their inner centre in meditation they often find insights into their lives and a way to come closer to their meaning, to their God. The dream, properly understood can lead us on our inner quest because the dream reveals a part of reality that He has created. God has created the physical world and the spiritual one. God gives us the dream as one way of discovering the nature of that world and our kinship with it.

Knowing something with the head is quite different from knowing something with the heart, knowing through experience. The latter kind of knowing gives certainty and knowledge. As we seriously consider our dreams, most of us can come to a relationship with the Dreamer within, the One who gives us the dream.[30]

To catch the dream, it is usually necessary to keep a paper and pencil at one's bedside. I find that alarm clocks and radios are almost a guarantee of dispersing a dream instantly. It is best to awaken naturally, steeped in the atmosphere of the dream, readied for appreciation of the gift.

A Sample Dream, 5 October 1986:
I was looking at some papers on a table. A glass of water fell over them. I wiped up the water and threw some wet pages out. I noticed a marker in the garbage (a paper-marker in the form of a cross. I had received the marker from someone special in my life). I quickly picked up the marker and tried to dry it, first one side, then the other. The second side was sticky. It kept sticking to my hands. I kept pulling it off – it

hurt! It tore my skin. I wanted to get rid of it. Finally I did. It fell into the garbage. I felt anxious.

- Work: (associations as told me by the dreamer)
  papers – information
    table – support
    water – life
    marker – reminder
    garbage – weight, junk
    pain – cross, faith
    skin – touch, sensitivity
- My Growth Life is definitely the subject of my dream.
- Interpretation: I wanted to grow but when I realised how much pain I would have to relive, I chose not to share.
- Now, two years later, I honour my dream by sharing as I can with the companions of my growth journey.

12

Fullness of Life

Few tools teach as effectively as the paradox. St Francis teaches: 'In dying, we are born to eternal life.'

For most people, I believe, the greatest disillusionment they will ever experience is the discovery that the moment of death is the most desirable of our lives. Death is a paradox. Truth lies in the paradox.

The only real death is death to the ego. The ego is not for control, but for identification. Hiding energies prevents life. I create a kind of hardness, a shell, a static state. I get stuck. This is death. The energy of life and love is replaced by fear, doubt, guilt, depression, apathy, anger, hopelessness. These things feel as though they are part of me, and eventually, they feel as though they *are* me. I believe them. I hold on to them, with a sense of holding on to at least *something*! At least, I *seem* happy with my negatives! I become attached to my fear, doubt, guilt, etc. To give them up would be to lose myself. It would mean to die. They become a pattern, a groove.

Death of ego brings enlightenment. This can be frightening for a person attached to ego energies. There is loss involved. I will have to empty places inside of me which are presently filled with illusions, such as sadness, pain, doubt, hopelessness. This requires the great risk of rejection! What if nothing fills my void when I share it?

To die in this sense requires faith that whenever energy flows out, energy flows in. This calls for faith and trust. Faith and trust are always rewarded, sometimes quickly and sometimes over a longer term, by changes in the person that can be described as radiance, lightness, etc. I become less emotionally heavy. The interior light has been turned on! This kind of death is never easy. There is always pain involved, and I let go of something I thought was myself!

'May your inner self grow strong' (*Ephesians* 3: 16). *There is no death*. This refers to physical death. In the *New Testament*, physical death is the point at which a person leaves the vehicle of his body which he uses on earth. After death we still experience the level of our love. If a person is afraid of death, it is because he has associated physical death with the loss of his ego-self or his deadness (this person is already dead!). This is understandable, because the ego lives in time. Our ego energies exist in *time*. . . it has a death. However, when it ends, a person comes to experience a reality that is endless, timeless, has no limits. Then and only then, does a person realise that death is not real![31]

John Main's treatment of the subject is similarly life-awakening: 'To have life in focus we must have death in our field of vision.'

Death reminds us of our fragility. It teaches us humility. At least dimly, we are aware that we need to make contact with eternal love, a love beyond measure, an undying love. Our mortal bodies need this new life. It is written within us that this is why we were created: 'infinite expansion of mind and heart.'

This is our way to go from mortality to new life. Jesus says: 'Unless the grain of wheat dies. . . ' (*John* 12: 24).

He refers to death of the ego, death to our self-importance, our exclusiveness, our limitations, our possessiveness. Because He has gone before, we can rise, too, to communion with Him, a life *sans* pain, *sans* darkness, *sans* fear.

This heaven is already at hand – for it happens within us. 'The Kingdom of God is within you!' (*Luke* 17: 21). The reign of God is present and anyone can enter it at any moment. The reality of the now, which is the only moment we have, enables us to share the peace, joy and love of Unconditional

Love. It is the starting point to which we must continually return. Heaven is the here and now. Heaven is my choice.

It was Albert Einstein who said, 'For us believing physicists the distinction between past, present and future is only an illusion, even if a stubborn one.'[32]

Paul says to us on the topic of Jesus' death:

> . . . we do see in Jesus one who was for a short while made lower than the angels and is now crowned with glory and splendour because he submitted to death; by God's grace he had to experience death for all mankind (*Hebrews* 2: 9).

Lawrence Freeman tells us that fullness of life is the purpose of our creation. This fullness is wholeness or integrity. Another name is holiness. 'It involves the integration of our tri-dimensional nature of body, mind and spirit because nothing is left out from the Kingdom except egotism.[33]

The ego is not bad, of course. It is necessarily part of the whole. But it is not to be identified with the true self. Egotism is a form of alienation. Alienation is hell. It results in suffering to myself and to those around me. It is in direct opposition to worship of the one true God. Reality lies with the true self, the fullness of which is experienced deeply within. 'The Kingdom of God is among you' (*Luke* 17: 21).

Our journey towards fullness of life is through our woundedness. Woundedness is common to all. It is a great gift to know the extent of our woundedness. To deal with this woundedness and to pass through it is to let go of the attraction it has for us. It is a privileged few who do take up the journey of reliving their pain. To relive my pain, to know its workings in me is death to the ego. This is the only death that is real!

Once I integrate my pain, it has no power over me. My woundedness does not disappear, no more than Christ's wounds disappeared after His Resurrection. But the sting is gone. 'Oh death! Where is your sting?' Death to the ego brings peace to the whole person. This is the 'Peace of Christ', that peace extended in the words of the Mass to every congregation around the world. This is the peace of the Resurrection. This is fullness of life. The journey is not completed while we have breath in our bodies. Thus, the process is a continuous beginning.

> Our destiny is not in this world, and we have to be prepared to go beyond death. We have to die to this world and everything in it, that is, everything that changes and passes in this world, to find the reality which does not change or pass.[34]

Our best preparation for this reality beyond the present world is the meditation. The chapter following offers us a way to move from the world of words to the realm of silence, from a kingdom of ideas to a lived experience, from a dealing of parts to immersion into a whole, from a peripheral rim to the centre of our beings. It is indeed a movement that fulfils the purpose of creation.

Bede Griffiths perceived the western world and the western Church as living from 'one half of our soul, from the conscious rational level.' He felt a need to discover the other half, 'the unconscious, intuitive dimension', so typical of the eastern world. He maintains that the future of the world depends on the marriage of the west and the east, the masculine and the feminine, the active and the passive, the conscious and the unconscious, the Yang and the Yin. It is this marriage that is deepened in us when we perceive the meaning of our existence. Contemplation becomes natural to our very soul, and death becomes the nuptial moment. We are admitted to the Feast of Life in its fullest.

'I came that they might have life and have it to the full' (*John* 10: 10).

13

The Transformer. . . Maranatha

The best way I know of discovering wholeness, the Kingdom within, the reality of my own infinity, is through Christian meditation. I quote the expert, John Main:

> Listen to the mantra as you say it, gently but continuously. You do not have to think or imagine anything, spiritual or otherwise. Meditation has nothing to do with quiet reverie or passive stillness, but with attentive wakefulness.
>
> If thoughts or images come these are distractions at the time of meditation, so return simply by saying your word. Don't use any energy by trying to dispel a distraction. Simply ignore it, and the way to ignore it is to say your mantra.
>
> Return with fidelity to meditation each morning and evening for between twenty and thirty minutes.
>
> Meditation is a pilgrimage to your own centre, to your own heart. However, we need faith and simplicity, and we need to become childlike. To enter into the simplicity of it demands discipline and even courage.
>
> If one is patient and faithful, meditation will bring us into deeper and deeper realms of silence. It is in this silence that we are led into the mystery of the eternal silence of God.
>
> That is the invitation of Christian prayer – to lose ourselves and to be absorbed in God. Each of us is summoned to the heights of Christian prayer, to the fullness of life. What we need, however, is the humility to tread the way very faithfully over a period of years so that the prayer of Christ may indeed be the grounding experience of our life.
>
> Meditation is a gift of such staggering proportions that we must respond to it gradually, gently. When we begin we

cannot understand the sheer magnificence and wonder of it. Each time we return to meditate we enter into that reality a little more deeply, a little more faithfully.

Because meditation leads us into the experience of love at the centre of our being, it makes us more loving people in our ordinary lives and relationships. Meditation is not only the necessary basis for contemplative action, but it is also the essential condition for a fully human response in life.

The wonderful beauty of prayer is that the opening of our heart is as natural as the opening of a flower. To let a flower open and bloom it is only necessary to let it be. So if we simply are, if we become and remain still and silent, our heart cannot but be open, the spirit cannot but pour through into our whole being.

It is for this we have been created.[35]

Who is John Main? He was born on 21 January 1926. Part of his student days were spent in London, England, as well as in Ballinskelligs, County Kerry, Ireland. He became a Benedictine monk with experience in journalism, and had lived as a soldier, and worked as a barrister.

In the spring of 1956, Main, who was then serving in the British Overseas Civil Service in Malaya, met a Hindu guru or swami, who taught him how to pray, using a short Christian prayer or mantra.

Years later, after his ordination, Main found to his surprise that the tradition of using this particular mantra for meditation went back to a Christian monk named Cassian. John Cassian lived in the desert near Cairo in the fourth century!

Cassian himself believed he was practising a form of prayer that went back to the early Church and which is found in the *New Testament* itself.

The mantra is a simple Aramaic word, *Maranatha*, and means, 'Come Lord'. It is a direct invocation of the presence of God at the centre of one's life and is repeated mentally over and over at regular times daily.

The object is to still the mind, block out all thoughts – even thoughts or images of God since these are bound to be inadequate or false anyway – and experience the true core of one's being. It is described as a way to find God in self and self in God. It is what the Hebrew Bible calls, 'waiting upon God'.

Main was meditating in this way for years, but it was only in 1975 that he formed a small prayer group at the Benedictine monastery in Ealing, London. In 1977, the Catholic Bishop of Montreal invited him to come and establish a priory to teach this form of meditation. By 1982, the year of his death, prayer groups had sprung up all across Canada, in Europe, Africa, South America, the United States, England and Ireland.

What is important is that this spreading movement involves rank and file people from all faiths. Ordinary folk, from housewives to factory workers, have learned to meditate from listening to Main's tapes or reading his books, *Word into Silence* and *Letters from the Heart*.[36]

Main was a lover of silence. He discovered that silence is the deepest language of one's being. One of his disciples, Lawrence Freeman, shares the following on this topic:

> True spirituality understands that silence can solve – and save – things at a level deeper than the reach of words. It even does so in less time than words, if there is the faith to sacrifice enough time to silence.
>
> Silence is an energy of interiority, not an evasion of externals. It conveys the source energy of God into human affairs more directly than any other medium. Nothing is more misguided than the idea of a society like ours, pre-occupied with the technology of communication, that silence is a vacuum demanding to be filled or an empty room waiting to be furnished. The meditator comes to know that of all the frequencies of communication, the Spirit is the most finely tuned because it is everywhere at once. Communication and response occur simultaneously in the Spirit's silent communion of presence.
>
> Silence is not a negation, absence or suspension of communication. (An angry or frightened silence is not true silence, but a nonverbal language.) It is the power that emanates from that communion – koinonia – which is the goal of all truthful

communicating. Silence is the simple, natural state of things. A person, or a thing, is silent when he is purely himself, without pretence, without even the self-conscious attempt to communicate himself.

Confidence is an attribute of silence. It is the confidence we re-acquire on the human level only when we have experienced God's simple, silent being with us. If we often fail to recognise God's presence, it is because we are looking for signs of communication rather than the evidence of communion. Until we have become simple again ourselves, we tend to be most suspicious of those with the least pretence. There is no image of God, other than the human person, because God is never more complicated than 'I am'.

Nature is silent because things in nature are simply themselves. This is what we mean by the word 'natural' and why we invariably use it in a complimentary sense. When Man denaturalises the environment to develop or exploit it, the power of nature to act as our closest friend and healer is polluted. Living in polluted and dehumanising cities intensifies the human need for the experience of wilderness for communion with nature in its unalloyed and unprettified purity and beauty.

The cliffs are not unsilent because of the roar of the sea or wind. Forests are no less silent for the sounds of the trees. By encountering the unconscious silence of creation, we are reminded of the silent consciousness of our human nature. Creation transmits the creating Word directly into human consciousness. The mind can wonder and seek languages to celebrate this awakening of the heart. It cannot reverse the order of events. The contemplative orientation towards life acknowledges the priority of the consciousness of the heart. The mind, in response, is attentive to the intelligence of the heart. It is to this habitual orientation that meditation restores us.

When we choose to follow the discipline of meditation we are committing ourselves to silence. To learn to be silent is to learn to be. St Symeon, in the tenth century, compared human knowledge of God to someone standing on the seashore at midnight trying to see across the ocean by the light of a small lantern. It is an image the meditator will understand in relation to the light of experience. Meditation is pure experience.

Reflection, poetry, theology are secondary. In the modern crisis of faith we have forgotten the priority of experience. Instead, we have come to think that faith, nurtured by religious thought and practice, leads to the experience of God. But it happens the other way around. As the first Christian teachers taught, it is faith that is generated by the experience of God. The experience is the gift of grace. And faith itself is a gift within a gift, hidden as it is revealed, as befits a mystery.

For this reason, sinners make the best contemplatives. We should never be too proud to admit to being contemplatives! Sinners are capable of a natural silence, an unpretentious way of being themselves. It is the righteous who pretend to be holier than they really are. The sinner's silence is gained, like the publican in Luke's gospel, by a simple acceptance of himself: a simplicity that repetition is needed to maintain. Such silence prepares us for the gift of that experience of God which initiates the process of conversion, and so of the journey of faith. However weak the light shed by the lantern of experience, it is enough to show that we are on the edge of the ocean of divine being that is lapping at our feet, and that it stretches far beyond our range of vision.

Freeman goes on to explain:

We have only to know one thing wholly in order to know everything. Consciousness expands when it has been concentrated to a single point of attention. Such concentration is poverty and the poor in spirit enjoy the vision of the pure of heart. If we fully enter the experience that we are given – the wave of the ocean that touches us as we stand on the sea's edge – we are immersed in the experience of the whole. Transformation is thus the result of concentration. And liberty is the grace of discipline.... The discipline of meditation leads the mind's eye through the darkness of all the purifying realms of silence. Then it releases that well of light which is liberty of spirit and the energy of peace.[37]

Lawrence Freeman also says that meditation is a tool whereby we find the God of consolation as opposed to the consolation of God:

God does not parentally pull the strings of our spiritual life but rather identifies Himself with our inconstancy and incompleteness. How then do we explain the alternation of light and shade? And, even more, how do we understand that this cyclical pattern does not preclude but actually motivates spiritual growth? A clue to this is found when the clouding over of the enlightened moment is caused by the attempt either to possess it or to articulate it. The meditator knows that as soon as he 'sees' his happiness he has begun to fear its loss and, therefore, to seek its possession. In a different dimension, outside meditation itself, we can endanger our stability on the path of analytical or over-enthusiastic description of it. To some degree this is an essential risk faith runs in witnessing to others and even a counter-balance to the possessiveness of a privatised spirituality – my own little garden where God and I walk alone. There are fine shades of meaning here. But we can say that what always tends to close the gates of the Kingdom and block the light is the objectification of the experience, whether by 'seeing' it in oneself or by encapsulating it in words or concepts. Prudent silence and non-possessive poverty, simplicity and mindful unself-consciousness are the natural conditions for realising the Kingdom. Because they are difficult to sustain, another factor is the essential: perseverance and regularity of discipline. Whoever endures to the end will be saved.[38]

14

The Way of Christian Meditation

The following is a synthesis of the teaching on Christian meditation by the late Dom John Main OSB, founder of the Benedictine Priory, Montreal, Quebec. It is designed specifically to assist newcomers joining a Christian meditation group.

Meditation involves coming to a stillness of spirit and a stillness of body. The extraordinary thing is that, in spite of all the distractions of the modern world, this silence is perfectly possible for all of us. To attain this silence and stillness we have to devote time, energy and love.

The way we set out on this pilgrimage is to recite a short phrase, a word that today is commonly called a mantra. This mantra is simply a means of turning our attention beyond ourselves, a method of drawing us away from our own thoughts and concerns. The real work of meditation is to attain harmony of body, mind and spirit. This is the aim given us by the psalmist: 'Be still and know that I am God'. In meditation we turn the searchlight of consciousness off ourselves. In meditation we are not thinking or imagining about God at all. In meditation we seek to do something immeasurably greater; we seek to be *with* God, to be *with* Jesus, to be *with* His Holy Spirit. In meditation we go beyond thoughts, even holy thoughts. Meditation is concerned not with thinking but with *being*. Our aim in Christian prayer is to allow God's mysterious and silent presence within us to become *the* reality which gives meaning, shape and purpose to everything we do, to everything we are. The task of meditation, therefore, is to bring our distracted mind to stillness, silence and concentration.

To meditate we seek a quiet place, and find a comfortable upright sitting position. Close your eyes gently. Sit relaxed but alert. Silently, interiorly begin to say a single word. We recommend the prayer phrase 'Maranatha'. It is utterly simple. Say it like this, MA-RA-NA-THA. Four equally stressed syllables. Some people say the word in conjunction with their calm and regular breathing. The speed should be fairly slow, fairly rhythmical.

Maranatha is Aramaic, the language Jesus himself spoke. It means 'Come Lord'. It is probably the most ancient Christian prayer. St Paul ends Corinthians with it, and St John ends Revelations with it. Listen to the mantra as you say it, gently but continuously. You do not have to think or imagine anything, spiritual or otherwise. Meditation has nothing to do with quiet reverie or passive stillness, but with attentive wakefulness.

John Main again emphasises the death to the ego that is the fruit of the disciple of meditation. He repeats essentially the same basic truths.

CHRISTIAN MEDITATION 'THROUGH THE WAY OF THE MANTRA WE JOURNEY TO THE HEART'

Meditation is not something new to the Christian experience. Rather it is central to the Christian experience and deeply rooted in Christian tradition. But many Christians have lost touch with their own tradition of prayer. We no longer benefit as we should from the wisdom and experienced counsel of the great teachers of prayer. All these teachers have agreed that in prayer it is not we ourselves who are taking the initiative. We are not talking to God. We are listening to the Word of God within us. We are not looking for God. It is God who has found us.

Walter Hilton expressed it very simply in the fourteenth century. He wrote: 'You, yourself do nothing, you simply allow Him to work in your soul.' The advice of St Theresa of Avila was in tune with this. She reminds us that all we can do in prayer is to dispose ourselves; the rest is in the power of the Spirit who leads us. St Paul wrote (*Romans* 8:26) that 'we do not know even how to pray, but the Spirit prays within us.' What this means in the language of our own day is that before we can pray we first have to learn to become still, to become attentive. Only then can we enter into loving awareness of the Spirit of Jesus within our heart.

Meditation, known also as contemplative prayer or deep prayer, is the prayer of silence and listening, the place where direct contact with the Christ within can occur, once the never-ceasing activity of the mind has been stilled. St John of the Cross said that the principal sign of readiness for silence in prayer was the awareness that discursive thinking at the time of prayer was a distraction and counter-productive.

THE TRADITION OF THE MANTRA

The mind has been described as a mighty tree filled with monkeys, all swinging from branch to branch and all in an incessant riot of chatter and movement. When we begin to meditate we recognise that description as a wonderfully apt portrayal of the constant whirl going on in our mind. Prayer is not a matter of adding to this confusion by trying to shout it down and adding more chatter.

The task of meditation is to bring the distracted mind to stillness, silence and attentiveness, to bring it into its proper service. This is the aim given us by the psalmist: 'Be still and know that I am God'. In order to assist us to come to stillness, we use a sacred phrase or mantra. It was John Cassian, who greatly influenced St Benedict, and who introduced the use of the MANTRA to western monasticism in the late fourth century. Cassian received the way of the mantra from the holy fathers of the desert who placed its origin back beyond living memory to Apostolic times and to the times of Christ himself.

Cassian recommended that anyone who wanted to learn to pray, should take a single short verse and just repeat this verse over and over again. In his Tenth Conference, he urges this method of simple and constant repetition as the best way of casting out all distractions and monkey chatter from the mind, in order that it might rest in God. When reading Cassian, one is reminded of the prayer that Jesus approved of when He tells us of the sinner who stood at the back of the temple and prayed in the single phrase: 'Lord, be merciful to me a sinner, Lord, be merciful to me a sinner.' He went home 'justified', Jesus tells us, whereas the Pharisee who stood at the front of the temple in loud eloquent prayer did not (*Luke* 18:9-14). The whole of the teaching of Cassian on prayer is based on the Gospels: 'When you pray do not be like the hypocrites. . . but go into a room by yourself, shut the door and pray to your Father who is there in the secret place. . . Do not go on babbling like the heathen, who imagine that the more they say, the more likely they are to be heard. Do not imitate them. Your Father knows what your needs are before you ask Him' (*Matthew* 6:5-8).

THE MANTRA ITSELF

There are various mantras which are possible for a beginner. However if you have no teacher to help you, you should choose a word that has been hallowed over the centuries by our Christian tradition. Some of these words were first taken over as mantras for Christian meditation by the Church in its earliest days. One of these words is MARANATHA. This Aramaic word means, 'Come Lord, Come Lord Jesus'. It is the mantra recommended by Dom John Main. It is the word which St Paul uses to end his first letter to the Corinthians (1 *Corinthians* 16:22), and the word with which St John ends the book of Revelation (*Revelations* 22:20). It also has a place in some of the earliest Christian liturgies. The Aramaic form is preferred because it has no associations for most of us and will help us into a silence that will gradually free us of all images.

Once you have chosen your mantra it is important not to change it. The reason for not changing the mantra you choose is twofold:

– If you keep to the same word always, it gradually becomes rooted in your deepest being as part of you, and it overflows into your whole life;

– If you change from one word to another it is like shopping around for something that works better, and thus expresses the self-concern that you are called to leave behind, the tyranny of whim and mood.

Begin to say your mantra and repeat it slowly through the whole period of your meditation. Once you have become aware that you have stopped saying the mantra, just begin again, without discouragement. Nothing is lost, no matter how often you wander off, so long as you begin again. In this way the restless movements of the mind, memory, imagination and emotions, are calmed and we are prepared for silence.

As you repeat your mantra you will find it acting like a plough, turning up the soil of your deepest consciousness to make it soft and receptive, and making a furrow of freedom and silence.

When we begin meditating it seems as though we are reciting the mantra in our mind, in our head, but as we make progress the mantra becomes more familiar, less of a stranger, less of an intruder in our consciousness. We find less effort is required to persevere in saying it throughout the time of our meditation. Then it seems that we are not so much reciting it, as sounding it in our heart. This is the stage that we describe as the mantra becoming rooted in our hearts.

The spiritual teachers of both east and west have always emphasised the essential importance of what they call the 'prayer of the heart'. They see the fundamental consequence of the fall as the separation of mind and heart in individuals. Indeed this sense of inner division pervades our contemporary self-understanding. The mind is our organ for truth; the heart our organ for love. But they cannot work independently of each other without filling us with a sense of failure, dishonesty, deep boredom or frenetic evasion of ourselves through busyness. Through the discipline of meditation we bring our mind and heart into a harmony that purifies and heals, clarifies our vision and opens our hearts ever more deeply to the Source of all Love that is within.

Meditation becomes a pilgrimage in which, in the depths of our heart, the Spirit speaks to our spirit through our life situation and the Word of God. Our part in meditation is to enter the stillness and to wait for Him there.

HOW TO MEDITATE

Sit down. Sit still and upright. Close your eyes lightly. Sit relaxed but alert. Breathe calmly and regularly. Silently, interiorly begin to say a single word. We recommend the prayer-phrase MA-RA-NA-THA. Recite it as four syllables of equal length. Listen to it as you say it, gently but continuously. Do not think or imagine anything – spiritual or otherwise. If thoughts and images come, these are distractions at the time of meditation, so keep returning to simply saying the word. Meditate each morning and evening for between twenty and thirty minutes.[39]

15

As I See It

'Much has been done to further human knowledge and skills, and the results are gratifying. But. . . much remains to be done to teach people the *art* of BEING. It is along the line of BEING and along that line only that solutions to mankind's basic problems will be found. The art of BEING is what our world needs, first to survive and then to live fully.'

I listened to these words in Athy in October 1989. Fr Pat Murray was the animator of a group who had gathered in the interests of growth and sharing. His perception 'As I See It' leads me to express the following about the topic of the 'Reconstruction of Persons':

● My best home for growth is *within myself.* I need to be at home with all of me. Even that in me which is not beautiful, that which is my 'hell' needs to be accepted. When I accept my hell, I am in heaven. Therefore every part of me must be welcomed.

● In matters of growth, there are no conscripts. The road proposed is one of (a) abandonment in faith to the God who created us; (b) abandonment, too, in faith to our own true selves created in the image of God and saved in Jesus Christ; (c) abandonment in faith to the journey companions that God has provided for us. Without this three-dimensional faith, the journey on the path of growth is impossible. Each one's journey is unique.

As faith is basic to growth, so it is basic to all healing and integration. When I *hurt* it is because I have been improperly revealed to myself – and I cannot, then, live according to my truth. The world of sin in which I was conceived, born and raised, has more or less marred me. I carry this world within me. I seek deliverance from this world because it weighs on me, is a burden on me. It makes me more or less blind, deaf, lame, at times aloof, and holds me captive.

It is only by mustering the life's strength within and around me that I will be able to penetrate this interior prison and come out of it purified of untruth, and healed of the pain inflicted by untruth.

● The TRUTH that sets us free is necessarily experiential, not just conceptual, truth. It has to be incarnated truth which will have penetrated my body, my feelings, my thoughts, and mainly my beliefs! Consciously or unconsciously, we adhere to a system of beliefs which operate automatically without *freedom of choice*. Growth and healing imply that we go beyond this automatic control system and learn (or un-learn) to rule our lives through free and deliberate choices. Free choice is a discipline. It is really a form of asceticism. Free and deliberate choices are the way to salvation. The healing is in the choice. . . for integration or disaster. Free-dom is the means to make the choice. If we stay with our defences, we die from them or live with them i.e. smoking, fear, anxiety, anger, alcohol, sexual exploitation. Then and only then, once the person has been reconstructed, commu-nity can happen!

● Reconstruction involves a difficult stage. The person who is loved is finally receiving what he/she has always wanted. Only slowly is it possible for the wounded person to believe in his/her good qualities. Anyone who has always lived in darkness needs time to adjust to the light.

Gradually, the richness of the in-depth zone emerges, becomes visible to the person in healing. Gentleness is dis-covered, and goodness and innocence, and each quality is claimed as the person is ready to own it. *What is, is*. Truth comes into focus. Cerebral and volunteeristic function pass to in-depth balance. In a few months, or years, depending on the extent of damage and other factors, re-construction is achieved. . . and the end result is more beautiful than the be-ginning!

Appendix

The following are a few excellent recipes from the Morris Center kitchen:

MORRIS CENTER MAYONNAISE
In blender:
2 Eggs
1 teaspoon Dry Mustard
Juice of 1 Lemon
Add slowly: 1¾ cups Safflower Oil – ¼ cup Linseed Oil

Allow blender to whisk mixture up white and fluffy before adding more oil. Add about ¼ cup of oil at a time until all is thoroughly blended.

* * *

TOFU DELIGHTFUL
Cut Tofu into slices ½ inch thick.

Place slices on a warm baking pan which has been lightly greased with Butter.

Marinate each slice with 5 or 6 drops of tamari sauce.

Heat tofu to about 250 degrees.

Serve warm as a protein with raw salad and lightly steamed greens.

* * *

AVOCADO DIP

In blender:
1 large ripe Avocado
½ cup hulled Sunflower Seeds
2 cups Water (more may be added if desired)
1 Garlic Clove, or ½ teaspoon Garlic Powder, if desired
Blend thoroughly. Serve as a vegetable dip or as a sauce.
Refrigerate until serving time.

* * *

NUTQUIK: A MILK SUBSTITUTE

In blender:
4 cups Water
Add: 1 cup finely ground Almonds
Blend until thoroughly liquified. Serve cold as a substitute
for milk.

* * *

WILD RICE

In covered cooking pot:
1 cup Wild Rice
4 cups Water
Bring Wild Rice and water to boil. Simmer slowly. Add more
water as necessary. Cook until rice is tender.
½ cup cranberries or raisins may be added just before rice
finishes cooking.

* * *

TOMATO KETCHUP[40]

12 medium ripe Tomatoes	1 teaspoon Celery Seed
1 large Spanish Onion	1 teaspoon Sea Salt
1 medium Sweet Red Pepper	½ cup Apple Cider Vinegar
1 teaspoon whole Cloves	½ cup frozen unsweetened
1 stick Cinnamon, broken	Apple Juice

1 teaspoon red Cayenne Pepper

Wash and trim vegetables and chop by hand, food processor or with the coarse blade of the food chopper. Put into a large saucepan, bring to a boil over medium heat, reduce heat and stir, for 15 minutes. Ladle a small amount at a time into a blender, and blend until as smooth as possible. Pour the puree back into large saucepan and bring to a boil over high heat. Reduce heat and simmer 30 minutes.

Tie cloves and cinnamon into a small cheesecloth bag and hang along with remaining ingredients. Simmer until very thick, at least an hour. Ladle into hot sterilised jars and seal immediately.

* * *

SPINACH OMELETTE

4 Eggs
1/2 pkg. of frozen or fresh Spinach
Dash of Sea Salt
Dash of Cayenne Pepper
1 tbsp. Butter

Beat egg yolks and whites in separate mixing bowls with fork or handmixer. Add salt and pepper to yolks. Then add cooked spinach to yolks and beat. Fold in beaten egg whites. Grease skillet with butter and pour in mixture. When it is brown, turn omelette over with spatula and heat until omelette appears firm. Serves 2.

* * *

HUMMUS

2 cups dry Baby Lima Beans
8-10 cups Water
1 tbsp. Lemon Juice
2 cloves Garlic
1/2 cup Safflower Oil

½ cup Apple Cider Vinegar
1 tbsp. Linseed Oil

Bring beans to a boil in water and simmer until well done. Drain water and save for soup stock. Beans may be thoroughly mashed or pureed in blender or Champion Juicer with 2 or more cloves of Garlic (to taste). Add 1 tbsp. lemon juice (fresh), ½ cup safflower oil, ½ cup apple cider vinegar and 1 tbsp. linseed oil. Mix well until hummus is of the consistency of creamy mashed potatoes. (Chick peas or other beans may be substituted – parsley or other herbs may be added).

* * *

SHAKE 'N BAKE CHICKEN (Morris Center Style)

Chicken, cut in serving pieces (remove all fat)
3 Eggs, whipped
1 cup Millet Flour
1 cup Buckwheat Flour
1 tsp. Poultry Seasoning

Sift together the millet and buckwheat flours. Stir in the poultry seasoning. Place in brown paper bag.

Dip each piece of chicken in the whipped egg, then into the paper bag and shake until chicken is well coated with flour mixture.

Oil a baking pan with soya lecithin oil and place the pieces of coated chicken on it. Leave uncovered. Preheat oven and bake at 325 degrees for 1 hour.

* * *

DRESSING FOR CHICKEN OR TURKEY

Basic recipe:
4 cups cooked Buckwheat, Millet or Mashed Potatoes
2 large Onions, chopped
1 or more cloves of Garlic
½ cup chopped Celery

1 chopped Apple (optional)
1 tsp. Poultry seasoning
Stock from the chicken or turkey may be added for moisture.
Mix all ingredients well and fill cavity of bird. Extra dressing
may be baked in a loaf pan.

* * *

BAKED STUFFED FISH

One whole Fish, approximately 3 lbs.
1 medium Onion, chopped
½ cup diced Celery
½ cup Butter
2 cups cooked Millet or Buckwheat
2 tbsp. chopped Parsley
1 dash Thyme
1 dash Sage
2 tbsp. Water
1 tsp. Sea Salt

Clean fish. Sprinkle lightly with salt inside and out. Cook the
onion and celery in the butter until tender. Combine with
remaining ingredients. Season to taste. Fill the fish cavity
with the stuffing and skewer sides together. Brush fish
generously with soft butter and coat with soya flour. Place
the fish in a pan lined with greased paper. Bake at 325
degrees in pre-heated oven allowing 15 minutes per inch of
stuffed thickness. Baste several times with a mixture of 2
parts water and 1 part butter. Place fish on a hot platter and
garnish with sprigs of parsley and lemon slices.

* * *

PIZZA

Line pans with pie crust and layer with the following:
Layer 1: chopped Eggplant
Layer 2: chopped Green Peppers
Layer 3: sliced tomatoes

Layer 4: sliced Mozzarella Cheese (reserve)
Bake at 325 degrees for 20-25 minutes. Add Mozzarella cheese. Reduce heat. Bake 5 minutes more until cheese is melted.

* * *

RATATOUILLE

$1/3$ cup Safflower Oil
2 cloves Garlic, chopped
2 large Onions, sliced
2 Zucchini, medium sliced
1 medium Eggplant, cubed (with skin on)
2 Green Peppers, cut in strips
.3 tsp. Potato Flour
5 ripe Tomatoes
1 tsp. Oregano
1 tsp. Vegetable Salt or Kelp
1 tsp. dried Dill weed
$1/10$ tsp Cayenne Pepper
2 tbsp. chopped Parsley
Heat oil in frying pan. Add garlic and onions. Saute until soft and transparent. Sprinkle potato flour over eggplant, zucchini and green peppers. Add to oil. Cover and simmer 1 hour. Add tomatoes and seasonings. Simmer uncovered until mixture is thick.

* * *

SNIP CHIPS (Snack)

Parsnip chips are a delicious alternate to potato chips. Cut parsnips in slivers. Dip in melted butter. Bake on a cookie sheet (stainless steel) at 320 degrees until tender. For crispness, bake longer.

If desired, frozen green peas may be added 5 minutes before parsnips are done.

* * *

TERRY'S BUCKWHEAT BREAD

3 Eggs
½ cup Safflower Oil
1 cup frozen Apple Juice (undiluted)
2 tsp. pure Vanilla
1 cup coarsely shredded Zucchini, unpared
1 cup shredded Carrots
1 cup Fruit Puree (either mashed Banana, raw grated Apple,
raw or canned crushed Pineapple)
4 cups Buckwheat Flour, finely ground
1 tsp. Baking Soda
3 tsp. Baking Powder (from Health Food Store)
1 tsp. Cinnamon
½ tsp. Nutmeg
1 ½ cups finely chopped Nuts

With electric mixer, beat 3 eggs to blend. Add oil, apple juice
and vanilla. Beat until thickened. With a spoon, stir in
shredded vegetables and fruit. In another bowl, combine
flour, soda, baking powder and spices. Stir flour mixture into
wet mixture just to blend. Add nuts and stir until blended.
Divide batter equally between greased and floured loaf
pans. Bake at 350 degrees for approx. 1 hour. Cool in pans for
10 minutes. Turn out on wire rack to cool.

   Variations: ½ cup peeled grated raw beets may be substituted for part of the shredded vegetables;
2 tbsp. carob powder may be added for flavour;
2 tsp. orange juice and chopped peel may be substituted for
vanilla.

* * *

ESSENE BREAD

2 cups Whole Wheat kernels
Pure Water for sprouting

Place wheat in a large glass jar. Add water until it is several
inches above the wheat. Cover mouth of jar with cheesecloth
and secure with an elastic band. Soak grain for 12 hours.

Drain water off through the cheesecloth and reserve liquid.*

Add more water through cheesecloth, rinse and drain. Place glass jar on its side so that the grain can have light and air. Allow kernels to sprout for 24 hours or until sprouts are ⅛" in length. Rinse with fresh water and drain three or four times during this 24 hour period.

Run the sprouted grain through your meat grinder. With wet hands, press and mould into a loaf. Oil a baking sheet or loaf pan with soya lecithin oil. Surface of bread may also be lightly coated with soya lecithin oil for a nice crust. Bake at 200 degrees for 3 hours or more. Bread should be covered with a glass or stainless steel bowl while baking. Makes 1 loaf. (A covered casserole is good).

*This water is called 'Rejuvilac' and contains many vitamins. Add to other juices for a nutritious drink.

Grain may need to sprout approx. 36 hours in winter months.

* * *

JOAN'S CHRISTMAS CAKE

2 cups Safflower Oil – 2 tbsp. Linseed Oil
6 Eggs
1 can frozen unsweetened Apple Juice
4 cups grated Carrots
1 pkg. frozen Cranberries
2 cups Apples (finely chopped) or unsweetened Pineapple
1 cup chopped Walnuts, Pecans and/or Sunflower Seeds
4 cups Buckwheat Flour
2 tsp. Baking Powder (double acting – from health food store)
2 tsp. Baking Soda
1½ tsp. Cinnamon
1½ tsp. Ginger
1 tsp. Allspice (optional)

In bowl or mixer, beat together the eggs, oil and apple juice. Add grated carrots and chopped apple or pineapple. In separate bowl, mix dry ingredients together thoroughly, flour, baking powder and baking soda, and spices.

Add slowly to the above wet ingredients. Beat well. Mix in nuts and cranberries. Pour into 4 or 5 loaf pans. Bake at 300 degrees for 1 hour. Cake is well done when an inserted toothpick comes out dry.

* * *

BANANA MILK SHAKE

4 ripe Bananas
1 Egg (or 2)
½ cup Whey Powder
½ teaspoon Pure Vanilla
½ teaspoon Nutmeg
2 cups Water (or more)
Peel Bananas and chill in freezer.
Combine egg(s), water and whey powder in blender. Mix well and add vanilla and nutmeg. Chop chilled bananas and add to blender. Serve cold. (4 cups).

Yogurt may be added for whey. Bananas may be partly frozen.

* * *

STUFFED DATES

1 pound of ripe Dates
Peanut Butter from Health Food Store
Remove pits from Dates. Fill cavities with peanut butter.

* * *

DANDY CANDY

2 cups Peanut Butter (Health Food Store)
2 cups Whey Powder
1 cup Carob Powder
½ cup Nuts (chop)
¾ cup frozen unsweetened Apple Juice
Sesame Seeds

2 tsp. pure Vanilla
2 grated Carrots

Combine peanut butter, whey powder, apple juice, and vanilla in bowl. Mix until ingredients are well blended. For fudgy candy, add carob powder. Add nuts. Shape into balls and roll in sesame seeds, or pat mixture into pan and sprinkle with sesame seeds. Cover or wrap in plastic-wrap and freeze for 1 hour. Cut candy in pan into bite-size pieces. Store in freezer.

Notes

1. Dr Leo Schafer of Unity, Saskatchewan, Canada was knighted in Denmark in 1987 in recognition of his outstanding work in the field of alternate therapy.
2. Additional beneficial information on this topic can be found in *Eat Right to Stay Healthy and Enjoy Life More* by Dennis Burkitt, MD or *The Fiber Factor* by *Prevention* staff. (*Prevention* is America's leading health magazine and is published in New York).
3. Hutchins, Alma R., *Indian Herbology of North America*, Merco, ON, Canada, 1973, pp. 67-68.
4. Jensen, Dr Bernard, *Pathways to Health and Disease*, 1981 (chart).
5. Bansal, H. L. & Bansal, R. S. Drs, *Magnetic Cure for Common Diseases*, Orient Paperbacks, Delhi, India 110006, 1983, p. 176.
6. Davis, Albert Roy, Ph D, *The Anatomy of Biomagnetism*, Schafer's Health Center, Unity, SK, Canada, 1979, 1980, 1981, p. 80.
7. Bansal & Bansal.
8. *Ibid.*, p. 24
9. Gleaned chiefly from *The Anatomy of Biomagnetism* by Albert Roy Davis and from personal experience.
10. Spiros Lenis, founder of the Hippocrates School of Nutrition, Delta, BC, Canada.
11. Lenis, Spiros, *Light Dynamics*, Lenis Ventures, Inc., Delta, BC, Canada, 1986, p. 75.
12. The light machines are available through Fetouris International, Ltd., 108a Boundry Road, London NW8 ORH

and Hippocrates School of Nutrition, 4501–96 Street, R. R. 3, Delta, BC V4K 3N3.

13. Quoted in *Nutrition News*, Canadian Nutrition Institute, Inc., Uxbridge, ON, Canada, May/June 1986, p. 4.

14. Lenis, Spiros, *Light Dynamics*, p. 40.

15. Quoted in CHOM *Newsletter*, Vol. 9, No. 2, Winter 1988/1989, p. 2.

16. Ford, Terra, *Schizophrenia Cured*, Brigden's Photo/graphics Ltd., Regina, SK, Canada, 1979, p. 105.

17. Hoffer, Abram, MD, Ph D, FRCP, CHOM Convention, Winnipeg, MB, Canada, 1984.

18. Diamond, Marilyn and Harvey, *Fit for Life*, Warner Books, New York, NY 10103, 1985, p. 27.

19. *Common Ground*, Toronto, ON, Fall 1985, pp. 4-5, quoting Dr John McDoughall, *The Case Against Milk*. Dr McDougall is Assistant Clinical Professor at the University of Hawaii Medical School and operates a private practice there. He is co-author of the bestseller *The McDoughall Plan*, New Century Publications, Inc., Tiscataway, NJ, USA, 1985.

20. CHOM *Newsletter*, Vol. 9, No. 2, Winter 1988/1989, p. 2.

21. Williams, R & Kalita, D., *A Physician's Handbook on Orthomolecular Medicine*, Pergamon Press, Toronto, 1977, p. 205.

22. *Ibid.*, p. 85.

23. Jensen, Dr B., *Iridology, the Science and Practice in the Healing Arts*, Vol II, Jensen Publications, Escondido, California, USA 1982, p. 438.

24. *Ibid.*, p. 458.

25. Main, John, OSB, *The Present Christ*, Darton Longman & Todd, London, 1985, p. 25.

26. Jensen, Dr B., *Iridology, the Science and Practice in the Healing Arts*, Foreword.

27. *Ibid.*, p. 371.

28. *Ibid.*, p. 454.

29. Trent, Michael, Homily on 'Feast of Christ, the King', 1988.

30. Kelsey, Morton, *Dreams, A Way to Listen to God*, Paulist Press, Toronto, 1978, pp. 100-101.

31. These points are taken almost word for word from a treatise on Death given by Fr Pat Murray in Galilee, Athy, Co. Kildare in January 1988.

32. Quoted in Jensen, Dr B., *Iridology, the Science and Practice in the Healing Arts*, p. 248.

33. Freeman, Lawrence, OSB, *Newsletter*, London, 20 December, 1988.

34. Griffiths, Bede, OSB, *The Marriage of East and West*, Templegate Pub., Springfield, IL, 1982, p. 203.

35. *Prairie Messenger*, 8 February 1988, p. II.

36. John Main's *Word Into Silence* is published by Paulist Press, New York and *Letters from the Heart* by Crossroad, New York. Both books are available from the Benedictine Priory, 1475 Pine Avenue W., Montreal, P.Q., Canada H3G IB3.

37. Freeman, Lawrence, OSB, *Newsletter*, 27 September 1988, pp. 6-7.

38. Freeman, Lawrence, OSB, *Newsletter*, 15 April 1988, p. 4.

39. Material from the Benedictine Priory, Montreal, PQ (see also no. 36).

40. Zemliak, Judy, *Naturally Yours*, Gateway Pub. Co., Ltd., Winnipeg, MB, Canada, 1985, no. 121.

Bibliography

Bansal H. L. & Bansal R. S., Drs; *Magnetic Cure for Common Diseases*, Orient Paperbacks, Delhi, India 110006, 1983.

Burkitt, Dennis, *Eat Right to Stay Healthy and Enjoy Life More*, Positive Health Guides, Arco New York.

CHOM *Newsletter*.

Common Ground, Toronto, ON, Canada, Fall 1985.

Cott, Dr Alan: *Doctors speak on the Orthomolecular Approach* Canadian Schizophenic Foundation Publication.

Davis, Albert Roy, Ph D; *The Anatomy of Biomagnetism*, Schafer's Health Center, Unity, SK, Canada.

Diamond, Marilyn and Harvey; *Fit for Life*, Warner Books, New York, NY 10103, 1985.

Ford, Terra; *Schizophrenia Cured*, Brigden's Photo/graphics Ltd., Regina, SK, Canada, 1979.

Freeman, Lawrence, OSB; *Newsletter*, London, England, 20 December 1988.

and *Newsletter*, Montreal, Canada, 27 September 1988.

and *Newsletter*, Montreal, Canada, 15 April 1988.

Griffiths, Bede, OSB; *The Marriage of East and West*, Templegate Pub., Springfield, IL, USA, 1982.

Hutchins, Alma R.; *Indian Herbology of North America*, Merco, ON, Canada, 1973.

Jensen, Dr Bernard; *Iridology, The Science and Practice in the Healing Arts*, vol. 11, Jensen Pub., Escondido, California, USA, 1982.

and *Pathways to Health and Disease* (chart), 1981.

Kelsey, Morton; *Dreams, A Way to Listen to God*, Paulist Press, Toronto, 1978.

Lenis, Spiros, Ph D; *Light Dynamics*, Lenis Ventures, Hippocrates School of Nutrition, Delta, BC, Canada, 1986.

McDoughall, John, Dr; *The McDoughall Plan*, New Century Pubications, Inc., Tiscataway, NJ, USA, 1985.

Main, Dom John, OSB; *The Present Christ*, Darton, Logman & Todd, London, England, 1985.

Nutrition News, Canadian Nutrition Institute, Inc., Uxbridge, ON, May/June 1986.

Williams, R & Kalita, D *A Physician's Handbook on Orthomolecular Medicine*, Pergamon Press, Toronto, 1977.

Zemliak, Judy, *Naturally Yours;* Gateway Pub. Co., Ltd., Winnipeg, MB, Canada, 1985.

PETER CALVAY HERMIT

Rayner Torkington

This is a fast moving and fascinating story of a young priest in search of holiness and of the hermit who helps him. The principles of Christian Spirituality are pin-pointed with a ruthless accuracy that challenges the integrity of the reader, and dares him to abandon himself to the only One who can radically make him new. The Author not only shows how prayer is the principal means of doing this, but he details a 'Blue Print' for prayer for the beginner, and outlines and explains the most ancient Christian prayer tradition, while maintaining the same compelling style throughout.

Over 34,000 copies of this bestseller have been sold.

PETER CALVAY

PROPHET

Rayner Torkington

This book is first and foremost a brilliant exposition of the inner meaning of prayer and of the profound truths that underlie the spiritual life. Here at last is a voice that speaks with authority and consumate clarity amidst so much contemporary confusion, of the only One who makes all things new and of how to receive Him.

More Interesting Titles

Body-Mind Meditation
A Gateway to Spirituality

Louis Hughes, OP

You can take this book as your guide for a fascinating journey that need not take you beyond your own hall door. For it is an inward journey, and it will take you no further than God who, for those who want him as a friend, lives within. On the way to God-awareness, you will be invited to experience deep relaxation of body and mind.

Body-Mind Meditation can help you become a more integrated balanced person. It is an especially helpful approach to meditation if the pace of life is too fast for you, or if you find yourself frequently tense or exhausted.

An Easy Guide to Meditation

Roy Eugene Davis

Meditation is the natural process to use to release tension, reduce stress, increase awareness, concentrate more effectively and be open to life. In this book you will learn how to meditate correctly for inner growth and spiritual awareness. Specific guidelines are provided to assist the beginner as well as the more advanced meditator. Here are proven techniques used by accomplished meditators for years: *prayer, mantra, sound–light contemplation, ways to expand consciousness and to experience transcendence.*

Over 100,000 copies sold.

THE WAY OF A HEALER

Peter Gill

Introduction by Lilla Bek

THE WAY OF A HEALER deals with different aspects of healing, and the way that spiritual healing works in the lives of people. Healing means health, and health is wholeness. That word wholeness implies a number of separate parts coming together to make a complete whole. We are accustomed to the concept of body, mind and soul, and unless these different aspects of ourselves function together in harmony we have disharmony or dis-ease. If that condition of dis-ease is allowed to continue unchecked, ultimately we have disease or illness. Spiritual healing works at the physical, mental, emotional and spiritual levels of a person.

Today we stand upon the brink of the darkest age that could yet befall mankind, or, with a change of consciousness, upon the edge of a new and wonderful dawn to herald in a golden age. What that age will be depends upon what we make of it now. The immediate need is for a concept which will integrate us with the life of the solar system and, through the solar consciousness, link us with the life of the universe and the word of God. Our thinking must become much more expansive to embrace, not only humankind as we know it, but also the angel, elemental and nature kingdoms, and other realms not normally perceived by our physical sense.